MAKING
FRIENDS
WITH YOUR
FATHER

MAKING FRIENDS WITH YOUR FATHER

A BOOK FOR DAUGHTERS

Kay Marshall Strom

ZondervanPublishingHouse
Grand Rapids, Michigan

A Division of HarperCollins*Publishers*

MAKING FRIENDS WITH YOUR FATHER
Copyright © 1992 by Kay Marshall Strom

Requests for information should be addressed to:
Zondervan Publishing House
Grand Rapids, Michigan 49530

Library of Congress Cataloging-in-Publication Data

Strom, Kay Marshall, 1943–
   Making friends with your father / Kay Marshall Strom.
     p. cm.
   ISBN 0-310-54891-8
   1. Fathers—United States. 2. Fathers and daughters—United
States. 3. Fathers—Religious aspects—Christianity. I. Title.
HQ756.S88 1992
306.874′2—dc20   91–42346
                                              CIP

Edited by Linda Vanderzalm
Cover design by David Marty

Printed in the United States of America

92 93 94 95 96 97 / CH / 10 9 8 7 6 5 4 3 2 1

This book is lovingly dedicated to
my father, Albert Marshall,
who first taught me about dad-daughter relationships;
to my husband, Larry,
who built a relationship with our daughter;
and to my son, Eric,
the future father of some lucky little girl.

CONTENTS

A Word to Daughters

My father is my friend. I respect him, and I admire him. I also enjoy his company. It wasn't always that way between us, however. Our friendship didn't come automatically. It was a process.

What is friendship anyway? That's a good question, especially when we use the term to describe the relationship between a daughter and her father. I once owned a little book entitled *A Friend Is Someone Who Likes You*. Not a bad definition for a word that is hard to define. Making friends with our fathers means coming to a point where we truly, honestly, genuinely *like* our dads.

If you are like most women, you are probably ready to declare your love vigorously for your father. "Of course I love him!" you say. "He's my *dad!*" But if one were to delve deeply into your relationship, to ask you specific and probing questions, it just might come out that you really don't *like* your father all that much. That's the way it is with many daughters. For you see, though *love* bears a close relationship to *like*, the two are not the same.

We daughters have heard and read a lot in recent years about mother-daughter relationships. Not nearly so much has been written about daughters and their fathers. Yet experts agree that the relationship each of us has with our father is pivotal to our successful progress into healthy, well-balanced adulthood.

Your father's influence on you began when you were very young. In those early days, you probably loved your daddy as only an adoring daughter can. But as you grew older, you began to see that your father wasn't as perfect as you had thought. And that's when the chasm may have begun to develop between you. Now that you are an adult, able to grasp reality and readjust to more realistic expectations, you may need to do some serious bridge building.

For each of us, the process starts with learning to understand: to understand yourself, to understand your past, to understand your father. It's also important to begin to see why your dad matters so much in your adult life. Because understanding is a fundamental cornerstone, it is the focus of the first part of this book.

Yet it's not enough simply to understand. Before change can take place, we must build on this foundation in definite, concrete steps. Building toward change, then, is the focus of the second part of the book. It begins with changing the effect your father has on you and learning to express both anger and your love toward him. Then comes learning to forgive him and learning to accept him—not for what you want him to be, but for who he is.

This book doesn't promise you a magic formula for either minor fence mending or major bridge building. And it doesn't offer any easy solutions to your long-standing problems with your father. I wish it could. But the fact is that healthy relationships don't come easily. Like any other worthwhile relationship, this one will require work and time and patience and determination. As we come closer to a clearer understanding of who we are, who our dads are, and how we relate to each other as daughters and fathers, we can begin to move forward toward a true and enduring friendship.

It is my prayer that the principles and suggestions in this book will help you find answers to some of the problems that have grown up between you and your dad. It is my hope that you will gain a whole new respect for your father, a better understanding of him, and a mature love for him. Most of all it is my hope and prayer that as a result of your efforts, you and your father will discover a more intimate friendship than either of you ever thought possible.

You can make it happen! To this end I wish you happy reading.

PART I.
LEARNING TO UNDERSTAND

1.

In the Beginning

Every woman on earth shares one common fact: Young or old, rich or poor, happy or sad, every single one of us is some man's daughter. We all have fathers.

But that's where the similarity ends. Some dads were good ones. Others were not so good. Some fathers were failures. Other dads left. Some stayed around but remained on the sidelines. Other dads became the most important people in our lives.

In the movie *Parenthood,* Steve Martin's character turns to his wife and says something like, "Remember when the kids were first born, and we hadn't done anything wrong yet?" That line must have struck a familiar chord in the hearts of every father who heard it. Poor dads! They start out knowing so little about the job of fathering. No wonder they make mistakes. If your dad erred in just small ways, it's probably not too hard for you to shrug your shoulders and say, "It's all right, Dad. I understand." But if your father was one who made really major blunders, you may find it difficult to understand and forgive.

Traditionally, fathers have been considered both the most important and the least important of our two parents. As wage earners, they were indispensable. But when it came to nurturing and caring for children, most of our fathers played second fiddle to our mothers. That's the way it was in my family. Dad brought home the bacon; Mom cooked it up and fed it to us kids.

Carrie, a thirty-two-year-old mother of two, reflects about her father. "I have two older brothers. From the time of my very first memories, Daddy treated me differently. He spanked my brothers; he just scolded me. He ruffled their hair and clapped them on their backs; he hugged and kissed me. I loved that part of being the girl in the family. The part I didn't like was Daddy's stubborn ideas about what girls should and shouldn't do. He always went to my brothers' ball games, for instance, but he never came to mine. He didn't like me playing on the softball team. I remember one time I ran crying into the house after getting hurt playing football with my brothers. When I went to my dad for comfort, all he said was, 'That's what you get for playing a boy's game when you're a girl.'"

While Carrie's memories are mixed, Linda lugs around bitter resentments. "My father provided for our family," says Linda. "We had a comfortable home and plenty of food on the table. But emotionally he gave us kids almost nothing. I guess he was like a lot of men of his generation. Loving and caring was Mom's job. I always got good grades, but my dad never said anything about it. He never came to my school programs or my piano recitals. When I remembered to do my chores around the house or took on something extra just to help out, he said nothing. No 'Good job, Linda' ever came from him. Hard work and success were simply what he expected of me."

Old memories, present regrets. Yesterday's hurts, today's resentments. These are feelings and emotions that should be in the past, but many of us can't seem to shake them. What does it all mean?

WHAT IS YOUR RELATIONSHIP TO YOUR DAD?

I haven't lived at home with my family for any significant period of time since the morning I boarded a

Greyhound bus in San Francisco and left for college in Santa Barbara. I was seventeen years old and felt ever so mature and sophisticated. I saw my father, on the other hand, as narrow-minded and provincial, and I was certain I had next to nothing in common with him. I had outgrown my daddy.

And yet at times I found I looked to him for help. I was quick to call on him when a boy I couldn't get rid of kept telephoning me. Dad hated making up excuses and abhorred "little white lies," but he stumbled through for me. I remember my father's smiles, hugs, and bursting pride when I graduated from college. "You're the first in our family," he told me again and again. Dad was so moved when my daughter was born that he wrote me a letter. To my knowledge, it's the only letter he's ever written. As the years go by, my father continues to play a part in my life.

Throughout the years that your life and your father's overlap, you two will remain deeply important to each other. Even when one of you dies, the bond between you will remain. You share a very special past, a part of life that is stored forever in your and your father's conscious and unconscious memory.

Your dad's importance to you arises from that shared history. Whether or not you realize it, you have profound feelings for your dad, feelings that bridge time and distance, conflict and change. Your feelings are probably a mixed bag of love and hate, pride and disappointment, respect and resentment. A great mixture of emotions works together to form the strands of the invisible cord that forever bonds you with your father.

The lucky among us have a positive bond with our fathers. For the less fortunate, anger, guilt, and even hatred form a bond so strong and so harmful that it can destroy both you and your dad. As you read this book, you will hear from women who have troubled, painful relationships with their fathers as well as from those women whose father-daughter relationships are a source of joy and fulfillment.

As I listened to women speak, as I read their letters, and as I sorted through their responses to questionnaires, I realized that my relationship with my dad has its positive and negative dimensions. That's the way it is with most of us.

HOW HAS YOUR FATHER INFLUENCED YOU?

"Like father, like daughter" the saying goes. Is that true of you and your dad? Experts agree it's not possible to understand a woman without first understanding her relationship with her father. Hidden within the past is the key to her fears, her needs, her strengths, her weaknesses, her dreams, her secrets. Within the shared history of daddy and little girl resides the key to the woman.

"My dad was a faithful man," Joanne reflects. "Faithful to my mom and faithful to his responsibilities to his family, church, and job. I see that characteristic in my own life. It's real important to me to be responsible and dependable in my relationships. I'm grateful that my dad modeled that characteristic for me."

"I want to be a good parent," says Linda, the mother of two. "I really do. So why do I keep doing so many things the way my father did? I hated those traits in my dad, and I hate them in myself."

"I don't believe in God anymore," Marla bluntly claims. "The last thing I need is another father."

My dad taught me to appreciate things around me. Tucked away among my memories are those special Saturday mornings when he would take my brother and me to work with him. We loved it! My dad was the manager of a bakery in San Francisco, and Dennis and I spent the day nibbling on cookies, sniffing at the oven doors, and hanging over the cake decorators. On the way home one Saturday, I bubbled, "Daddy, for my birthday, I want a chocolate cake with frosting roses!"

Several months later, on my tenth birthday, my dad

presented me with a chocolate cupcake with vanilla frosting. On top was an enormous, intricate red rose. "I made it myself," he told me with that twinkly smile of his.

Think again about your dad's influence on you. List five positive influences:

1. _____

2. _____

3. _____

4. _____

5. _____

Have you ever thanked your dad for his influence in these areas? Consider talking to him about them or writing a note expressing your gratitude. You'll make his day!

Now list five specific areas of negative influence your dad has had on you.

1. _____

2. _____

3. _____

4. _____

5. _____

Take time to reflect about each of these areas. In what ways can you break that negative influence? Do you blame your dad for how you turned out? Now that you are an adult, who is responsible for the negative behaviors you see in yourself? If breaking your dad's negative influence is important to you, write down some steps you can take to move beyond this influence. Remember, you can't change your dad, but you can change his effect on you. We'll look into this possibility more closely in chapter 7.

Choice of Men

It was your dad who introduced you to the opposite sex. Whether you knew it or not, your father carefully taught you about masculinity. The direction those lessons took is evident in how you interact with the men in your life. Your father has had an indelible influence on your perception of men and your expectations of how they should behave toward you.

Therapists recognize that a woman's choice of men will be strongly influenced by her father and her relationship with him. They explain that human beings instinctively seek to repeat the patterns of their childhood, at least for a time, because those are the relationships that feel "right" to us.

That's why so many children of alcoholics end up marrying alcoholics. Women who grew up in abusive homes often become trapped in abusive relationships. Christian women whose fathers had no use for church often marry men who find no place in their lives for a spiritual dimension. On the other hand, women who grew up in an atmosphere of open sharing find that communication comes easily, and women who were raised by godly men tend to look for husbands who walk with God. What is familiar feels comfortable.

"My father was a real Peter Pan type of person," says Lonie. "He couldn't grow up. He was really sweet and charming, but he couldn't accept the responsibility of a family. He was always leaving us. My childhood was dedicated to trying to get him to accept me. I took piano lessons and practiced hard because he loved the piano. I always asked my teacher for pieces from Rogers and Hammerstein musicals because I knew that's what my dad liked the best. All through college I dated men very much like my father—fun loving and undependable. When I was nineteen, I dated a hippie-type professor who was thirty-two. He had blond, curly hair, and a receding hairline, just like my dad did."

Lonie was ambivalent about her father. She saw his weaknesses. Over and over she was hurt by his irresponsible behavior. Yet what she was always looking for was another daddy. "Thank goodness my friends had more insight and wisdom than I did," Lonie continues. "My roommate, who had visited in my home and met my dad, confronted me about my choice in men. I ended up marrying a man who is charming and fun, yet very different from my father in all the right ways."

"My own father had his faults," says Beth, "but he was as loyal to my mother as a Saint Bernard. I, in turn, never could abide men who flirted, cheated, or ogled. Once I noticed my boyfriend staring at an attractive woman in a bathing suit. I didn't feel jealous or threatened, and I had no desire to try to get his attention back to me. All I felt was an overwhelming urge to cut my ties to him—as soon as possible."

There is an important lesson in all of this: If you are lucky enough to have a great relationship with your father, you're going to have high expectations of men. And you probably won't settle for less. If, however, your father set a different kind of male role model for you, you will need to be on your guard as you establish relationships with men. When you are with a man who is important to you, ask yourself:

1. In what ways is this man like my father?
2. In what ways is he different?
3. What are the problem areas I see ahead for us?
4. Can I live with those things that irritate me, or am I counting on being able to change him?

Be especially careful not to involve yourself unwittingly with a repeat of the problems you had with your father.

WHAT ARE YOUR EXPECTATIONS?

Remember Robert Young in the old "Father Knows Best" television show? Now there was one successful dad.

He worked hard and provided well for his family. Yet he always had time to shoot a few baskets with Bud or to hold Kathy on his lap and soothe her tears or fears. He called his daughters "Princess" and "Kitten," and he was free with hugs, smiles, and encouraging words. He was always a paragon of wisdom and an unfailing source of patient understanding.

When you think of a successful father, do you have a Robert Young type of person in mind? Let me guess: Your father doesn't measure up to that picture. Mine doesn't either. That's because we live in real life.

It's unfair to pile a burden of unrealistic expectations onto our fathers' backs. In televisionland, any problem can be worked out in half an hour, and every situation can have a happy ending. But real life has no perfect fathers, and for many people life has no neat, happy endings.

What are your expectations of your father? What were your expectations when you were a young girl? How have they changed?

To understand how your dad measured up to your expectations, take a few minutes to reflect. Think of five times when your father failed to meet your expectations for him. List them here:

1. _____

2. _____

3. _____

4. _____

5. _____

Now ask yourself, *How did I feel each of these times?* Beside each event, jot down a few descriptive words or as much as several sentences. Now read through your list again. Considering each situation from an adult point of view, do you really think your expectations were realistic?

In each case, what was the result of placing blame on your dad?

Here's how I worked through this exercise: I remember when I was in seventh grade and my father promised he would be home from work by five o'clock to drive me to a junior-high dinner at church. I had made a gelatin salad in a fish-shaped mold and had carefully decorated it with olive eyes, cucumber scales, and a pimento mouth. Then, gelatin fish in hand, I sat by the living-room window to wait. I waited and I waited. Five o'clock came and went, but no dad. I waited. Six o'clock came and went. I waited. At about 6:15 my father finally pulled up. By then my fish was melting, and most of its scales had slid off. I got into the car and sat in stony silence all the way to church.

By the time I arrived, the tables had been cleared. "Kay, you're late!" my friend Carol shouted, and everyone turned and stared at me. I wished I could have disappeared through a crack in the floor. I was certain everyone was laughing at me and my dripping gelatin fish.

How did I feel? Indescribably embarrassed. Let down by my father. Unimportant to him. Foolish in front of my friends.

Looking back from an adult point of view, I know my expectations may have been unrealistic. My father had to work late, and he was the only driver in our family and had the only car. I don't recall any explanation from him, but I do recall not being in any mood to listen to one. What was the result of placing blame on my dad? I remember coming to the definite decision that I couldn't depend on my father to keep a promise.

How about your expectations? Are you demanding more from your father than you have a right to expect of him? Your relationship to your dad is influenced by four dynamics:

1. Your father's view of who you should be.
2. Your view of who you are.

3. Your view of who your father should be.
4. Your father's view of who he is.

Conflict and anger flare up when

1. You aren't living up to your father's expectations.
2. You've had it with trying to live up to them.
3. Your father isn't living up to your expectations.
4. He has had it with trying to live up to yours.

I know what you're thinking. You want to love your father just the way he is. And he probably says the same thing about you. But the fact of the matter is, feelings are *conditional*. That's just how we are. We can deny that we set conditions and claim that we have godlike love, but most of the time that just isn't reality.

So what's the answer? First, stop insisting that your love for your father is without conditions. Admit that you do have expectations, that you do set requirements. Acknowledge that your father has conditions of his own.

Once you have accepted this, try to determine exactly what those conditions and expectations are. "I could get along with my father if he wasn't so stubborn," you might say, or "If I really knew he loved me, I could love him." Or, "If he was a Christian, I could accept him."

Finally, work toward loosening the iron grip of those conditions and expectations. You may be pleasantly surprised to find that simply by admitting the conditions exist and by recognizing what they are, you will begin to move toward accepting your father *in spite* of what you perceive as his failures. So he's stubborn. So he isn't good at demonstrating his love. You can love him anyway. As for his relationship with Christ, accepting your father is the best thing you can do to help him see his need of God.

WHERE ARE YOU NOW?

Assess where your relationship with your dad is now. Do you lack a special closeness with your father? Have you always wished for a better relationship with him? Do you feel that something isn't quite right between you? Do you have a smooth surface relationship but without a real, harmonious relationship underneath? Or are things worse than that? Perhaps you two don't even speak.

Like Linda, you may sometimes wonder if the words you speak are yours or if they are his. Sometimes you may listen to yourself—if you're a parent, especially when you're talking to your kids—and you hear your dad's expressions, his words, his tone of voice. It can be scary.

When you do things differently from how your father would do them, are you worried about what his reaction will be? Are you so afraid that you quickly switch back to his way of acting, carefully convincing yourself that what your father expects of you just happens to be exactly what you want for yourself? And how about your dad? Even though you may be sure he loves you, do you now and then detect a tone that makes you wonder if he too might feel things could be better between you?

How Much Repair Work Does Your Relationship Need?

The following questions can help you decide how much mending and rebuilding your relationship with your father needs.

1. Are you free of anger and resentments against your father?
2. Do you feel relaxed when you and your dad are together?
3. Do you really enjoy your father's company?
4. Can you effectively communicate with your father?
5. Can you confide in him?
6. Can he confide in you?
7. Do you feel loved and accepted by him?
8. Are you able to look realistically at your father—at

his strengths and his weaknesses as well as at his triumphs and his failures?

9. Are you able to build a relationship with your dad without trying to change him?

10. If your father were to die suddenly, would you be able to accept his death without becoming all tangled up with resentment, guilt, and regrets?

If you were able to answer a quick and honest yes to every one of these questions, your relationship with your dad is probably in pretty great shape. (Of course, if that were the case, you probably wouldn't be reading this book in the first place.) But if you had some problems with your answers, you have work to do.

The next five chapters will help you come to a clearer understanding of who you are, who your father is, and how you relate to each other. Based on this understanding, you can begin to change your father's effect on you, express both your anger and love to him, forgive him, love him for who he is, and move together into a true friendship.

Making friends with your father is a personal challenge. Are you willing to accept it? The payoff is well worth the time and effort you will invest.

The road to friendship begins with understanding the past. And that's just where we will begin in chapter 2.

2.

Understanding the Past

My dad just left for home after spending almost a week at my house. The first five days were nice. He fixed the cuckoo clock and the sliding door. He helped me with my car, and he advised me on what to plant where in the garden. We had lunch together, and we watched television. On the sixth day we talked.

Dad and I talked for hours. He told me about an incident that happened when he was a young boy. He had been playing with a little toy truck in the construction area in which his father and older brother were building a new house for the family. My dad's mother called him in to take a nap, and by the time he got back outside, the house wall was up and his truck was sealed forever inside it. "I begged my father to take the wall down and get my truck," Dad said. "He didn't even answer me."

I talked about the fire that had destroyed my family's home six months earlier, and my dad told me about the fire that had destroyed his house and all of his belongings when he was eleven. He talked about the twelve-string guitar for which he had worked so hard and saved so carefully and waited so long. He had owned it only a few weeks before the fire destroyed it. "I cried when I realized it was gone," Dad admitted quietly.

My father told me a lot of other things that day, and I felt closer to him and loved him more than I ever had before. Maybe that was because I now knew him better. Maybe it was because, after so many years, I was finally catching a glimpse of who he used to be.

Understanding the past. That's a good place to begin.

Elise speaks freely of the pride her father took in her: "I was his golden-haired darling." Throughout childhood she was the center of his attention, favored over her three brothers. But that privileged relationship ended abruptly when Elise entered adulthood. "My dad was too lazy to make a go of his business," she said. "I worked with him and tried to help, but no one could tell him anything." According to Elise, she and her dad haven't had anything resembling a calm, pleasant conversation for over twenty years. Only now, well into her forties, is Elise beginning to understand some of the events that contributed to making her father the man he is.

PAST PATTERNS OF RELATING

The relationship that exists between a girl and her father is a strongly personal one. No one father-daughter interaction is exactly like another. Relationships can vary a great deal even within the same family. And the relationship can and often does change with time and circumstances.

Yet some general categories tend to emerge again and again. Look at the following descriptions of relationship patterns between dads and young girls, and see if you recognize your own past pattern of relating to your dad. By looking at how you related to your dad when you were young, you may better understand your present relationship.

Daddy's Girl

Kelly was a real daddy's girl. He doted over her, and she could do nothing wrong in his eyes. He lavished her with attention, marking all of her birthdays with wonderful gifts, bigger, more expensive, and more elaborate each year. "One year my dad flew me to San Francisco for dinner, just him and me," she bubbled. "While we were there, he took me shopping and bought me a diamond bracelet. He couldn't really afford it, but that's how much he loves me."

Kelly's pattern of relating to her dad has affected her relationship to males. As a young girl, she went through dozens of boyfriend-girlfriend relationships, none of which lasted longer than a few months. Even now she judges all men by the gifts they give her. If she doesn't get a big present, the guy is history. One guy made the fatal mistake of forgetting Valentine's Day. Another remembered, but sent "cheap" flowers instead of long-stemmed, red roses. Another had the audacity to give her "just a book" for her birthday. "Can you imagine?" Kelly says, shaking her head incredulously. "A book! What kind of a birthday present is that?" Kelly isn't at all uncertain about what she sees as the relationship between gifts and caring. "If a guy can't remember special days, he must not care much for me," she says with conviction.

Were you a daddy's girl? If so, you may find that establishing your independence from him is your main relationship problem.

Competition with Mom

Some father-daughter relationships are defined not so much by the father or the daughter as by the mother. Some moms take great pains to keep their daughters from bonding too closely with Dad. If you had such a mother and if she was successful in her efforts, you may have been prevented from having with your dad the kind of relaxed, sharing experiences that are so important to growing up happy and healthy.

Why would a mother come between her daughter and husband? Sometimes it's because she sees her daughter as competition for her husband's affection and attention. She may actually be jealous of her daughter. A mother who destructively competes with her own daughter for Daddy's attention is herself a little girl emotionally, one who feels woefully inadequate compared to others.

Do you remember feeling a competition between your mom and you for your dad's attention? How did you handle that competition? What effect did it have on your relationship to your dad?

Unaccepting Dads

Betsy spent most of her childhood trying to gain her dad's acceptance. She tried in the only way she knew how: she got good grades, won contests, and did well in sports. But she never felt her dad accepted her or approved of her. He never complimented her, never went to any of her games, never recognized her skills.

"Here I was, an honor student, a star athlete, and a competent person, yet without his acceptance I felt so insecure and worthless," she reflects. "Just a casual recognition that I existed and that I had value to him would have meant so much to me. Even just listening to me when I talked to him would have helped me feel loved."

Did your father show you he accepted you? Did he show interest in things that were important to you? Did he encourage your gifts and skills?

Defiant Daughters

Looking back on her childhood, Molly sees herself as a defiant daughter. "My father always had an opinion about everything, and he always let me know what he thought about most things I did. I found myself always taking the opposite point of view, just to prove I could do things my own way. When he told me to prepare for secretarial school because that's all he figured I could do, I fought his idea and prepared myself for a successful career in business."

Molly prided herself on having a mind of her own. What she didn't recognize was that by dedicating herself to defying her father, she was keeping him securely positioned in the number one slot. Her father wasn't keeping control of her. She was relinquishing control to him.

Do you remember fighting your dad, keeping him at a distance because you had something to prove? Did you spend a lot of your relational energy in arguing rather than in understanding?

The Ever-Pleasant Daughter

Many women grew up believing that it was their responsibility to be consistently and unremittingly agreeable, charming, and pleasant to their fathers. Carla said, "If I wasn't interested in what my dad had to say to me, it was my job to pretend I was. Father had to be charmed, conquered, and somehow won over to my side. If I failed to accomplish this, I was doomed to be forever unsuccessful with men. That was the unwritten rule in my family."

As a result of this one-sided, somewhat deceptive pattern of relating, Carla never got a chance to get close to her dad or to know him very well. Everything had been kept to superficial pleasantries. What appeared to be a harmonious relationship was actually a destructive and unfulfilling pattern.

Did you have an honest relationship with your dad? Or did you feel as if you always needed to please him and be agreeable?

Scary Father

"When I was little, I was scared to death of my father," Evelyn recalls. "He was so big, so strong, so loud. He never really hurt me, but he sure did scare me. One time, when I was five, he had put down a new sidewalk outside our house. I didn't know anything about wet cement, except that it was nice and squishy to walk in. So that's what I did, with my pet chickens behind me. When my dad discovered our footprints in his sidewalk, he was livid. I heard his bellowing and swearing, and I dove under my bed to hide. Dad got the broom and jabbed at me, trying to get me out. I was sure he was going to kill me. The funny thing is, I can't remember what happened after that. I don't think I even got a spanking. But I sure do remember the terror I felt."

Were you afraid of your father? What about him made you afraid? Looking back on your childhood from an adult perspective, were those fears warranted? Have those fears crippled you as an adult?

THAT WAS THEN, THIS IS NOW

Mark Twain once said: "When I was a boy of fourteen, my father was so ignorant I could hardly stand to have the old man around. But when I got to be twenty-one, I was astonished at how much the old man had learned."

Many daughters could echo this sentiment. Only for many, the awareness didn't come until the woman was much older than twenty-one. "I have come to realize a wonderful thing," Molly reports. "It's not my father I dislike. I dislike his way of controlling me. Once I realized that, my anger toward him no longer made any sense. He can't control me unless I let him. He may try to, but I'm now a competent adult, and I can handle my father's bossiness."

That's not all Molly discovered. "You know what?" she added. "On an adult-to-adult basis, I admire many things about my father. I think we really could learn to enjoy each other."

Although Molly's new realizations didn't lead to an instant change in her reactions to either her father or his dictates, they did allow her to begin to move in that direction.

Whatever has passed between the two of you when you were growing up affects your relationship, but it no longer needs to cripple it. You're now an adult, with adult perspectives, interacting with another adult—your dad. You can choose to break those old patterns of relating. You can give up being daddy's girl. You can move away from a pattern of defiance. You can choose to lose the power of those childhood fears of your dad.

As an adult, you can choose to replace fear with understanding, defiance with love. You can't go back and change the past, but you can make good choices about the present and the future.

WHAT DO WE DO WITH OUR MEMORIES?

Memory. What a selective thing it is. Take Lorraine, for instance. She wistfully recalls all the times she and her father went out together to select just the right Christmas tree. (She forgets about their inevitable bickering, her dad arguing that the tree she chose was too expensive, that she never did know the value of a dollar. Her return charge was that he was a cheapskate.) Lorraine talks warmly of her family's traditional Christmas Eve drive through the surrounding neighborhoods to look at the Christmas lights. "It was such a happy time," she recalls with a smile and a sigh. "Daddy driving, my mother sitting next to him, and all us kids in the back seat squealing with delight." (She forgets about her dad's irritation with their noise, his frustration with the traffic, and his anger at her mother's constant efforts to improve his driving.)

Sound familiar? Our memories are often incomplete and distorted. We forget the circumstances that surrounded those past "happy events." To one degree or another, we all suffer from distorted memories. Some of us tend to polish up and sugarcoat events from the past. Some of us do the opposite. We recall everything in a harsh, critical light. "Maybe," said Deborah when her counselor reminded her of her tendency to do this. "But I'm sure my memories of the way my father constantly humiliated me and verbally abused me are accurate. Just ask my brother and sister. They lived through it too."

Perhaps Deborah's memories are accurate. But she, like each of us, has a choice. She can continue feeling victimized by her father's behavior toward her, or she can recognize that his anger and hurt and actions are his own problem. She can choose a more appropriate and effective response to her father. You can do the same with yours.

LOOK AT YOUR DAD'S PAST

Each father is a product of many different influences. His innate personality, his parents, his siblings, his talents and disabilities, the people with whom he came in contact, the methods he chose to adapt to situations in his own life, the environment in which he was raised—all these factors helped to make him into what he is today.

I remember the exact moment I first began to look differently at my dad. My husband and I had taken a trip to the Ozark Mountains in Missouri and had stopped by the tiny town of Fordland, where my parents grew up. We were sitting in my father's Aunt Ollie's living room. I had never met any of the relatives from "back home," and I was thoroughly entranced with the stories of little Albert (my father). He was a tiny, sickly little boy. ("When he was born, he was so small he could fit into a shoe box. A silver dollar would cover his whole face.") He was the dependable older brother of a boisterous bully. ("Herb would get himself mixed up in all kinds of things, then he'd run to Albert for protection. Whenever your daddy fought, it was to rescue Herb.") My father's father was a circuit-riding preacher who governed his family with strict rules. ("He made those boys toe the line, all right.")

A picture began to form in my mind, a picture of the boy my father used to be. I nodded and smiled as I listened to Aunt Ollie's stories and began to comprehend this man I had lived with all my life.

The more you can learn about your father, the more you will be able to understand why he is the way he is. How much do you know about your father? If possible, talk to relatives or friends who "knew him when." And certainly set aside a time to talk to your father about himself. You might ask him questions like these:

1. What was your happiest childhood memory?
2. What was your saddest?
3. What was the scariest thing that ever happened to you?
4. What were your parents like?
5. How did you get along with them?
6. What do you remember most about each of your brothers and sisters?
7. Are there things in me that remind you of yourself?

Almost any dad likes to talk about himself, especially when someone is really interested in listening.

Whose Job Is It Anyway?

"Why does the weight of having to understand always fall on me?" you might ask. "My dad doesn't even try. If he won't do his part, why should I?"

Because that's the only way it will work. You can try to understand your father, but you can't control what he does.

Joseph Joubert wrote, "A part of kindness consists in loving people more than they deserve." Perhaps this applies to you and your father.

SO WHAT'S THE END RESULT?

Your father is your father, and he always will be. The influences he brought into your childhood have become a permanent part of you. Choose to pull out all the good and healthy and positive things that passed between you and your dad in those early years. Search out the love and caring and support and respect. These can become both your best defenses and your best offenses in life.

The women with the most confidence are, almost invariably, those who were treated as valued people when they were little girls. Perhaps you don't feel you were one of the lucky ones. When you were young, your father may not have stood beside you and cheered you on. Pause now to take a harder look at him. Dig a little deeper into your memory bank. See what evidence you can find to indicate that he truly did care about you.

"My dad had such a temper," says Aimee. "When he got angry—which was often—I was terrified. That's pretty much how I remember him, irritable and angry. That's why I was so surprised one day when I was looking through some old family pictures and found one of my father carrying me on his shoulders. He was smiling, and I was laughing and holding on to his ears. There was another one of the two of us and a big German Shepherd. Evidently I was afraid of the dog, because I was crying and clinging to my dad. He was holding me close. Then there was one of him teaching me to ride my bike, running along beside me, looking proud as I wobbled along. Suddenly I began to remember a different side of my father, the side of him that really loved me, the side that really cared, the side I had forgotten."

You saw your father through special and prejudiced eyes. That's how it is in a family. You can't filter out very much. Dwight L. Moody once said, "A man ought to live so that everybody knows he is a Christian . . . and most of all, his *family* ought to know." That's the hardest task of all.

Some dads were not very good at leaving a positive mark on their families. Now that you're an adult, try to give your dad the benefit of the doubt. Determine to take along with you the things about him that were the best and the most affirming, and toss aside the negative.

GET READY

You've done a lot of remembering. Sometimes that's a hard thing to do. But it's the remembering that leads to the understanding, and it is with the understanding that healing starts.

In the chapters that follow, you will find not only information and suggestions for bridge building and fence mending but also practical strategies you can apply to your own situation. Before we consider our different dads in chapter 3, ask yourself these questions:

1. What have I learned about my father?
2. What have I learned from him?
3. In what ways am I a product of my relationship with my father?
4. In what ways would I like to change some of the results of that relationship?

You might want to share your answers to questions 1 and 2 with your father. He may be surprised and touched at how important he is to you and how successful he was in passing along the things he considers important. Hold on to your answers to questions 3 and 4, however. We will be considering those issues as we progress through the next chapters.

3.

Our Different Dads

Each dad is different. Each is a unique blend of strengths and weaknesses. And that unique blend of characteristics affects who you are and what your relationship with your dad will be like.

When your relationship hits rough spots, it's easy to say, "If only my dad would change, our relationship would be so much better." Again, forget trying to change your dad. That approach won't help.

What may help, though, is trying to understand how your dad's strengths and weaknesses affect you. This chapter will look at several types of father figures. You may see one that resembles your dad.

FATHER FIGURES

What is your dad like? How would you describe him? What kind of a father figure does he represent?

Dads Who Give a Legacy of Love

"My parents had two boys. Then I came along," Carrie says. "To my father, I was perfect. So perfect that he didn't want to have any more children. For him, the family was complete with me. I've heard that story of my dad and me many times, and I must admit it never fails to fill me with joy."

A legacy of love from a father. What a way to start life! "Dad was my hero," Carrie continues. "He taught me to hit a baseball. He took me on bike rides. He went to every one of my piano recitals and sat in the front row and smiled and cheered. Never did I doubt his love for me. He carried my picture around in his wallet and showed it to everyone who would look. 'This is my daughter,' he'd boast. 'She looks just like me!' "

In a perfect world, every daughter would feel as secure in her father's love as Carrie does. In the real world, however, many daughters just look on enviously.

Dads Who Are Overly Protective

Some loving dads have a tendency to be overly protective of their daughters. It's hard for a caring father to distinguish that fine line between being lovingly protective and smothering his daughter.

"He wouldn't let me do anything," Tricia says of her father. "Every time I'd complain about having to miss a Sunday picnic with my friends or turn down a date with some guy my father didn't know, my dad would recite his favorite line: 'I do it only because I care about you.' How I had wished he cared a little less!"

Overprotectiveness runs the gamut from the trivial ("My dad wouldn't let me wear skirts above my knees.") to the extreme ("I couldn't leave home to go to college."). Some surpass the extreme ("In my dad's eyes, no boy was good enough for me. I didn't have my first date until I was in college.").

The results of an overprotective father usually take one of two directions. Either the daughter cooperates ("I stayed home and went to our local community college.") or she rebels ("The minute I got to school every day, I rolled up my skirt until it was the shortest one on campus."). Sometimes the results are disastrous. ("I knew so little about dating, I was a pushover for any guy who looked at me. I got pregnant on my very first date.")

Dads Who Play Favorites

"I know it's unfair for a parent to prefer one child over another," Carrie says. "But I have to admit that I always enjoyed knowing that my dad loved me best."

That's great for Carrie, but what about daughters who aren't the favorite?

"Most fathers would probably insist that they don't have a favorite child," Diana says. "I know my dad always denied it. But he did have a favorite, and it sure wasn't me."

Every young girl harbors the secret hope that her father loves her best. But being the second best—or worst of all, the never loved—can be the most painful and destructive feeling a child can be called on to endure. Even if Dad denies it. Even if the charge isn't true. Even if there is a good reason for Dad's closer relationship with one child than with the other.

Whether we like it or not, some personalities simply mesh together more comfortably than others do. "My dad and I always got on each other's nerves," Diana says. "Everything I did irritated him. It was different with my sister. She was Daddy's pet."

It is almost impossible for an "unfavorite" daughter to grow up with a strong positive relationship with her father.

Dads Who Are the Big Boss

The big boss father makes his guiding rule clear from the beginning: *I am boss!* And he never lets his family forget it. If you are the daughter of a big boss, you never have any question about where you stand. Boss dads say such things as: "Don't *tell* me where you're going. *Ask* me."

If you had a boss for a father, you know how this kind of dad operates. His word is law. His desires and his comfort come first. He demands obedience and respect from his children. Under no circumstances do his kids question or argue with his rules.

"In my family, my father was the boss supreme," Deborah remembers. "He gave the orders, and we kids jumped to obey." After a pause she adds, "Even when we were young, my brother, sister, and I reacted to my dad differently. I fought. But my sister, she went along with everything he said. As for my brother, he became a miniature copy of my dad and joined in on giving orders. Dad liked that. Guess which one of us suffered the most? Right. Me."

If your father was a boss-type dad, how did you relate to him? Did you fight him as Deborah did? Did you surrender to him like her sister? Or did you join him? Almost certainly you took one of these three stances. It might surprise you to know that the style of coping you chose probably has had a lot to do with the way you now relate to other people.

"Give me an order," Deborah admits, "and I want to rebel. When I see a fifty-five-mile-per-hour speed limit posted, my foot immediately presses down on the accelerator, and I go sixty-five. When I see a sign that tells me to stay off the grass, I go out of my way to walk across it."

If you decided to stand up to your boss dad, you probably have become a real fighter. Your growing-up years may have been one battle after another, showdown following showdown. You were defiant. You were punished. You simmered and dreamed of revenge. It may be that out of your battles you have developed a grudging respect for your father. Or maybe your anger and resentment simply hardened into a cold distancing that persists to this day.

How about the surrender route? If you chose this path, you probably have a different kind of difficulty. "While he fought with me," Deborah says, "he humiliated my sister.

The harder she tried to obey, the higher he raised the requirements. I remember one time she wanted to go to the beach with her friend's family. Dad said she could go after she washed the dishes. But when he inspected the dishes, he found some that weren't perfectly clean, so he made her wash every dish over again. When she finished, he inspected them again and found one tiny spot. So she had to wash the entire stack over again. This happened four times. By the time my dad finally let her go, her friend had left. My sister spent the rest of the afternoon on her bed crying."

If you have surrendered too much of yourself, you may find that it's now almost impossible for you to be firm and assertive to anyone about anything. In your life, your dad is still the boss.

"My brother became like a 'little boss,' " Deborah continues. "I remember how he used to go through the house and snatch up anything my sister or I had not put away and hide it. Then he'd make us pay to get our things back. Dad thought Joey was pretty smart to think of holding our stuff hostage."

It's nice to be on the winning team. It feels great to be aligned on the side of strength. It's secure there. When a girl learns just what it is that the boss wants, what qualities he admires, and how she can get rewarded for emulating him, "little boss" becomes an attractive option. A person who aligns herself with her father quickly learns the advantages of being aggressive, egotistical. and domineering—as long, of course, as she doesn't make the mistake of challenging her dad's authority.

If your dad is the big boss, are you a fighter? Do you surrender? Do you align yourself with him? What are the consequences of your choice—in your relationship to him and others? What are you prepared to do to change your situation?

Dads Who Are Weak

Some fathers are weak, wishy-washy, ineffective, unassertive, and often subordinate to their wives. In this dynamic, a daughter grows up feeling she can't depend on her dad. If he is morally weak—or if she sees him as such—how can he help her develop her own moral guidelines?

If you are the daughter of a weak father, you may feel it's your duty to fix him. Feeling driven to complete the task of fixing their own fathers, many daughters of weak fathers repeatedly seek out weak men to take their dad's place.

If your dad is weak, try to relate to him on the basis of his strengths rather than his weaknesses. The first step in doing this is to quit trying to make your father strong. The next step is to quit resenting him for what he is not.

Dads Who Are Out of Control

"My earliest memories are of lying in bed at night, listening to the screaming and banging coming from my parents' room," Linda says with an almost icy hardness to her voice. "One time, when I was about nine years old, I tiptoed out of my room and saw my father threatening my mother with a pair of scissors. I was sure he was going to kill her. I made my way to the telephone in the hall, intent on calling the police. But my father saw me. He grabbed the telephone out of my hand and smacked me across the face with it."

Chapter 4 will discuss the specific problems faced by women who, like Linda, lived with problem fathers. But I think it's important also to recognize here those of you who struggled to grow up with fathers whose behavior was out of control. At best, your relationship with your dad is probably strained. At worst, it is nonexistent.

"I thought I'd outgrown all that old resentment," Linda says. "Many times I was certain I was finally ready for some sort of relationship with my father. Again and again it was my intention to somehow begin to communicate with him, to find some common meeting ground. It never happened. Each time I'd tell myself, 'Forget it. He isn't worth it.' But I couldn't forget it. I've never quit trying."

Most of us didn't grow up with a physically violent father. But many of us lived with emotional violence. Many fathers frighten and intimidate their children even though they never lay a hand on them. Our society is just beginning to recognize the tremendous damage done by parents who subject their children to this environment we call emotional abuse.

Whether your out-of-control father showed his anger with his fists or with threats or insinuations, the effect on you may be the same. "It wasn't that my father abused me physically," Corrine says. "It's just that whenever he was around, he would call me names or yell at someone in the family. I always felt like a nothing around him. I still do."

To one degree or another, every family uses guilt and intimidation in their relationships with each other. The variables are the degree of the manipulation and an individual's response to it. Part of making friends with your father is learning to change his effect on you. We'll look at that more carefully in chapter 7.

YOUR ROLE MODEL

Carrie's father served as a role model for his daughter. So did Deborah's father and Tricia's and Linda's and Diana's and Corrine's. They were not all good models for their daughters, but they were models nonetheless.

"I always saw my dad reading the Bible," Susanna says. "If the church doors were open, he was there. Dad didn't actually talk to me much about God or about his own faith, but there was never any doubt in my mind as to where he stood. I could see it in his life."

"A real honest-to-goodness church man," Linda says.

"That was my father. Everyone at church thought he was the greatest. But then, they didn't have to live with the hypocrisy in his life. As for me, I have *nothing* to do with *any* church. I'm not at all sure I even believe in God anymore."

What is your father like? What are the characteristics that make him unique? See if you can choose a few of his strongest traits to use as building blocks for the new, healthy, positive relationship you are preparing to build.

4.

Problem Fathers

It was Marianne's seventh birthday, and she couldn't wait for school to be over. Her daddy was coming to get her. Over and over she had told everyone who would listen all about their plans. Together she and her father were going to go miniature golfing. After that they were going to a pizza parlor for pepperoni pizza, her favorite. Maybe after that he would take her to a movie, just the two of them. Before they went home, her dad had promised they would stop for an ice cream soda.

When the bell rang to signal the end of school, Marianne ran out the door and over to the flagpole. That's where her dad had told her to meet him. With her back pressed against the flagpole, Marianne waved to her friends as they left for home.

"Have fun with your dad!" they called out.

"I will," she promised.

Marianne waited and waited and waited. To help pass the time, she picked a bouquet of wildflowers to give her dad when he came.

As her teacher left for the parking lot late in the afternoon, she called out, "Are you still here, Marianne? Maybe you should go on home."

But Marianne shook her head. Her dad was coming to get her. He had promised.

By the time the sun began to set over the mountains,

Marianne, shivering in her thin sweater, could no longer deny the truth. Once again her dad had let her down. She flung down her handful of drooping flowers and stomped them into the ground. Then, with tears of anger and frustration running down her face, she slammed her lunch box against the flagpole with all her might. The top popped off and her pink-checked thermos smashed to the ground.

By the time Marianne's father finally staggered into the house, the birthday girl had been in bed for hours. Her father stumbled up to his daughter's room and dropped onto her bed beside her.

Marianne pretended she was asleep.

Her father took the little girl's hand in his and pressed a shiny new silver dollar into it. In the slurred speech so familiar to Marianne, he whispered, "I'm sorry, Honey. I got tied up. Happy birthday."

Marianne turned her back to him.

For a minute Marianne's dad sat quietly beside her. Then, in a surprisingly steady voice, he said, "I may not be much of a father, Marianne, but you might as well love me because I'm the only father you've got."

Fathers come laden down with all kinds of problems, some of them devastating. If you grew up with a problem dad, you may live with great pain and deep scars. You may be wrestling with tremendous problems of your own, difficulties that can be traced directly back to your father's problems.

It's easy for those who haven't walked in your shoes to say glibly, "Let bygones be bygones" or "Forgive and forget" or "That happened long ago when you were just a kid. It's time you grew up and forgot it."

"Most people thought I came from a normal, run-of-the-mill family," Deborah says. "Dad was a minister, and Mom stayed home with us kids. Dad was very religious, and he was a strict disciplinarian, two traits many of our family's friends admired. Dad was also a child molester. No one outside the family knew about that."

For years Deborah suffered in silence. Then came the day she discovered that her younger sister was also a victim of her dad's abuse.

"That's when I approached my mother," Deborah explained. "I couldn't stand to see Sarah going through what I had gone through."

What did her mother do?

"Nothing," Deborah says bitterly. "She acted as if it was my fault. She didn't say it in so many words, but she made it perfectly clear that if I kept quiet, I wouldn't be punished. So I kept quiet."

The list of damaging emotions and responses suffered by Deborah, Marianne, and others like them seems almost endless: guilt, shame, rage, anxiety, low self-esteem, fear, sexual problems, loneliness, eating disorders, compulsiveness, a lack of trust, obsessions, repeated victimizations, a driving need for control. If you grew up with a problem dad, you undoubtedly have scars of your own you could add to the list.

"Every aspect of my life has been affected," Deborah says sadly. She may well be right.

As an old Chinese proverb says, "In a broken nest there are few whole eggs." If you were raised in a dysfunctional family, you probably have not escaped unscathed. You may have compensated in amazing ways. You may have come through surprisingly intact. Your wounds may have healed, and your scars may be well hidden. But you were damaged. And the scars remain.

On that devastating night of Marianne's seventh birthday, she considered her father's words to her. What he said was true, she decided. He *was* the only father she had. Before he left her room, Marianne slipped her arms around his neck and hugged him.

DYSFUNCTIONAL FAMILIES

If you were raised in a healthy family that expressed acceptance, openness, building up of each other, communication, love, and caring, you are a blessed woman. If not, you will need to work extra hard in order to develop a positive relationship with your father.

How did your family measure up? Did your father offer you the love and security you needed? Did he encourage you and build you up? Did he teach and guide you? If you were raised in a dysfunctional family that was marred by alcoholism, emotional or physical abuse, rejection, or other emotionally crippling dynamics, you may have entered adulthood feeling needy and fearful and distrustful.

In *Always Daddy's Girl*, H. Norman Wright explains it this way:

> Imagine that your life is represented by a cup. When you were born your cup was empty. You had a lot of needs which had to be met. If your family was healthy, most of your needs were met, and when you reached adulthood your cup was full or almost full.
>
> But if your family wasn't healthy, your cup may only be a fourth, a sixth or an eighth full. You entered life with needs which your father and your family should have met, but didn't. The lower the level in your cup, the more you tend to try to fill it from the outside, often with compulsive or addictive behavior.[1]

Marianne's family was undoubtedly dysfunctional. We understand the problems in a family where there was abuse or molestation. What we sometimes miss is the damage incurred by a more insidious type of abuse, fathers who fail to see and accept their daughters as worthwhile people. This type of father's pervasive attitude is

- "You aren't good enough."
- "You never do anything right."
- "There are two ways to do it; my way and the wrong way."
- "Children are to be seen and not heard."
- "I lay down the law, you obey it."

Do you recognize your father in any of these? It may be that you also suffered from a degree of dysfunction in your family. Whether your family's dysfunction was blatant or insidious, I have good news. You are not a prisoner of your past. You need not be forever crippled by having grown up with a less-than-perfect father.

You may be convinced you have no shred of love left for your father. Don't be too sure. You may be amazed at what is buried deep down in your heart. Love doesn't die easily. You can't erase the past, but you can move forward.

God, the Great Physician, can heal you. And however broken your life may be, he can rebuild it. "Yet, O Lord, you are our Father. We are the clay, you are the potter; we are all the work of your hand" (Isa. 64:8).

Your heavenly Father knows all about the damage done to you by the problems of your earthly father, and he is able and willing to repair it all. It's up to you. Are you ready to commit yourself to the remolding of your life? Perhaps some of the following chapters will help you on the road to healing.

No More the Rescuer

If your dad is a troubled person, it's very natural for you to want to rescue him. It feels like the Christian thing to do. You want to help him.

You may have already fallen into the role of the rescuer. You find yourself defending him. Making excuses for him comes naturally. You may even be accustomed to going a step farther and playing peacemaker between him and your mother. You find it feels good to have your family turn to you for help, to depend on you. Playing the part of the rescuer allows you to believe that you really can hold everything together.

But understand this: If you play the role of rescuer, you can expect to be frustrated. And you can expect that frustration to grow into anger, maybe even rage. Expect to get to the place where you will throw your hands in the air and cry, "I give up! You're beyond help!" But don't expect your family to let you quit. Once you take on the rescuer role, everyone else will fight hard to keep you right there rescuing. Even if they would let you quit, you would find it hard to give up the rescuer role.

One of the first steps toward healing the effects of a relationship with a dysfunctional father is to refuse to play the rescuer. It may be frightening finally to admit and accept the fact that you really can do nothing for your dad. And yet it's the truth. You *can't* change him. You *can't* be an effective rescuer.

No More the Victim

Some women play the role of helpless victim. But beware: To accept this role is to refuse your own healing because by nature the victim perceives that something bad is always happening to her. Your constant theme has to be, "Look, Dad, at what you've done to me!"

Not that there isn't a payoff for the victim. Victims get a lot of attention. When they are angry or resentful, they can claim a righteous justification for their feelings. They can wrest a degree of revenge from dad by building on his sense of guilt. And, perhaps strongest of all, they can avoid the terrifying responsibility of taking charge of their own lives and going through the painful process of mending and healing themselves. The victim's theme is "It's not my fault."

If you play the victim, your dad benefits too. He can always point to you as his "thorn in the flesh." He can blame you for his problems. In you he can find a distraction from other, more threatening issues that he doesn't want to face. If you allow yourself to play the victim, you will stay miserable indefinitely.

STEPPING OUT OF YOUR CHILDHOOD PATTERN

Changing family roles is an extremely difficult thing to do. Our old responses are deeply implanted in us, and the roots go back to the beginning of our lives.

But change is possible. It begins with recognizing the role you are playing. Once you see where you are, you will be able to take action and make a change.

1. Decide what you want to change. Be specific. Instead of saying, "I don't want to let my father get to me," say, "I no longer want to pretend that my father's rudeness doesn't bother me."

2. Refuse to respond to him as if you were still his little girl. You can be a victim only if you allow yourself to be victimized. If your dad bellows, "Do it the way I told you to!" you can respond with a matter-of-fact, "You may be right, Dad, but I'm going to do it differently this time."

3. Don't move too fast. It has taken you many years to develop your role. Don't expect it to change overnight. To suddenly announce, "From now on things are going to be different around here," whether by word or by action, will confuse your father and put him on the defensive. It will be easier for you to be patient and to head off resistance if you move slowly and deliberately.

4. Set realistic goals. No matter how determined you are to make changes, you will sometimes slip back into your old way of doing things. When that happens, don't let it destroy your resolve. Concentrate instead on the progress you are making.

5. Do it! It's easy to get so wrapped up in talking and planning that you never get around to acting. Only action will bring results.

6. Be flexible. If one approach doesn't work for you, try something else. No one method will work for everyone. You need to find what will work for you. Again and again, episode after episode, year after year, Marianne had struggled to break out of her rescuer role. She tried to talk to her father, but it always ended up the same—with her accusing and her father defending. Every time Marianne grew frustrated and every time her dad grew angry. She finally had to admit that, however much she wanted it, all her efforts and all her talking were never going to work.

On her father's sixty-fifth birthday, Marianne wrote him the following letter:

Dear Dad,

Instead of a store-bought card with flowers or ducks or footballs, this year I'm making you a birthday card. I want to wish you the happiest birthday of your whole life, and I want to do it with my own words.

Just as it happens in every other family, an awful lot has happened to us over the years. It makes me sad that there is such a deep, deep chasm between us. Whose fault is it? Both of ours, Dad—yours and mine. You were drunk too often. Your irresponsibility and unreliability caused me great pain. But I played a part too. I purposely blocked any possibility of a relationship between us. You never really knew me, Dad, and I never knew you. I kept it that way.

But that was in the past. Now I want things to be different between us. It was true what you said all those years ago. You *are* the only dad I have. And, yes, I do love you. In spite of everything, in spite of myself, I think I always have loved you.

Things are changing, Dad. I haven't seen you drunk for over two years. But change comes slowly, and you know how impatient I always was. While we're waiting for the changes in each other, let's really try to get to know each other as we are right now. Let's enjoy each other whenever we can. When we can't, let's at least agree to do our best to get along. Let's really try to understand each other better. It will make it so much easier for us to love each other as we should.

Happy birthday, Dad.

Love,
Marianne

Marianne's father lost no time in replying to his daughter's birthday letter. That evening a dozen red roses arrived for her.

"We have a long way to go," Marianne readily admits. "But I now feel better about my father and me than I have ever felt in my entire life."

Even if your father doesn't cooperate, you can be successful. Deborah is finding her own way out of her anger and resentment. "After two years of counseling," she says, "I have come a long, long way. Even though my father and I aren't any closer together, I no longer feel anger and bitterness toward him. And I know God will continue to heal me of my past."

OTHER ROLE MODELS

An especially frightening side effect that hounds many daughters of problem fathers is this: They are afraid they're doomed to carry on the painful legacy passed down to them. "My secret fear is that I'll end up like my father," says Marianne. "When I look at my father, I see myself. We have the same dark brown hair, the same pale, freckled skin, the same light blue eyes. We are both artistic. We like the same movies, and we laugh at the same jokes. We're too much alike."

You need to understand a great and freeing truth: The die is not cast against you. You can make your own decisions about your life. You can determine to emulate the best in your father, and you can reject the worst.

You may be able to make changes on your own. If not,

don't hesitate to enlist the help of a qualified counselor. Also, surround yourself with positive role models who can demonstrate what you weren't able to learn from your father.

"When I was ten years old, I spent a lot of time with my friend, Kathy," Deborah said. "For the first time in my life I saw a caring father at work. Later on I visited quite a bit with my aunt and uncle. I watched the carefree, comfortable relationship Uncle Walter had with my cousins. Through Kathy's dad and my uncle, I discovered that another way was possible, a way of faithfulness, loyalty, kindness, and godliness."

MOVE FORWARD

"I can't think of any happy memories from my childhood," Marianne says with more sadness than bitterness. "My father's main influence on my adult life is to make me determined not to become like him. Sure, my husband and I have our problems. But they are nothing like the ones I saw when I was growing up. And I have resolved to keep it that way."

Then, her voice softening still more, Marianne adds, "I understand my father better now. He never had a positive role model when he was growing up. I'm not making an excuse for his behavior, but knowing about his childhood gives me a better idea of how these patterns work in families. I no longer have to be angry and to resent him because I know he was addicted to alcohol. His actions were nothing personal against me."

"I have a long way to go," Deborah admits. "But one thing I know for sure: The legacy of molestation and abuse in my family stops right here with me. My husband, our children, and I are starting a new family legacy—one built on a foundation of love, respect, trust, and communication. Our children will never grow up the way I did. They will never know the horribly sad feeling of having absolutely no one in the world they can trust."

God is sovereign. He can and does heal the most devastating of injuries. However weak you started out, you can through his strength have the courage and endurance to be strong. You can learn to trust again. You can learn to love.

5.

Dads Who Weren't There

"My father adored me, and I worshiped him," says Helen. "At least that's what my mother tells me. I can't remember. Daddy died suddenly when I was three."

"I know it sounds awful," Julia admits quietly, "but when I was growing up, I used to pretend my father was dead. It seemed easier to accept his death than the truth— that he left us for another woman and her children."

For more and more daughters, the problem of making friends with their fathers is complicated by the fact that their fathers weren't around when they were growing up.

Growing up without a father is hard. Even when there's another man around to call Dad, even when a father determines to spend quality time with his daughter, even when his wife doesn't run him down. Even when everyone makes the best of the situation, it's still hard for a girl to grow up without her father at home.

Whether it's harder to lose a father through death or through divorce has been the subject of many discussions and studies. Most people assume that it's easier to come to terms with a dad who died than one who is absent because of divorce and that it's easier to accept a stepfather if the real father is no longer around. Actually, the opposite seems to be true. Several studies indicate that children whose fathers had died resented their mother's new husband more than did children whose parents were divorced. Surprised?

It's easier to understand when we consider some of the reasons compiled from the results of several research projects. They suggest that:

1. Mothers tend to remarry more quickly after a divorce than after a husband's death. This longer intermediate time allows more time for a child to become comfortably settled into life alone with Mom.

2. A daughter is more likely to idealize a father who died. When a widowed mom remarries, her daughter often perceives the marriage as an act of disloyalty to a dad who is not only blameless but also unable to defend himself.

3. Children of divorce tend to be younger than children whose fathers have died. Younger kids adapt more easily than older ones do.

4. Children whose fathers have died can't run back to their dad's house when things get tense and rocky at home. They have little choice but to stay and work out the problems.

A father doesn't have to be dead or divorced to be absent. Many fathers who live with their daughters have abandoned them emotionally.

Was or is your dad absent from your life? How do you cope with this loss? If he is still living, how do you relate to him in these circumstances?

ABANDONMENT

"My father left for work one morning and he never came home," says Ginnie, her voice tinged with pained bitterness. "He just left. Grandma got a couple of post cards from him, but my mother and us kids never heard a word. He just walked out of our lives and slammed the door shut behind him."

The most difficult situation is presented by fathers who abandon their daughters, either literally or psychologically. It's tough to have to come to terms with a dad who seems to have no thought or concern for his own child. Daughters whose dads have died or are separated or divorced may feel rejected, hurt, angry, resentful, unloved, guilty, and confused, but they can at least catch a glimpse of the other side of the coin. That isn't true for the daughter who has been abandoned. For her, there is no other side. With such blatant and complete rejection, she sees little room left for hope.

Ginnie tells poignant stories of the intense feelings of loss and depression she felt when her father deserted the family. "But before long those feelings were replaced by a resentment that has grown deeper and deeper through the years," she says. "How could he have walked out on us like that? How could he have left without ever even saying goodbye?"

Since it's hard for children to express or even feel anger toward their parents, they often decide their dad's desertion must be their fault. "For a long time I was convinced that I had done something awful and that was why he left," Ginnie says. "Now I know I had nothing to do with it. Yet even now, way back in the recesses of my mind, that guilty feeling hangs on."

Depression, difficulty in handling aggression, and guilt are common traits in children whose homes are broken by separation and divorce. They are even more common—and are felt more strongly—in abandoned children.

Many mothers decide the best way to protect their children is to tell them their dad left because "he is sick" or because "he has something wrong with him." Mom's reasoning makes sense. And to some degree it's true. Without a doubt a father who deserts his family has a problem that may well verge on illness. But according to experts, such an explanation makes it harder for a child to show or recognize her resentment and anger toward her father. Too often she ends up turning those unresolved feelings against herself.

There is no perfect way for a mother to explain a father's desertion to her daughter. About the best a mom can do is to assure her child, "None of this is your fault. You did nothing to cause it. Your father left because he had a problem he couldn't handle." It's also helpful to add, "What he did was wrong."

A sensitive mother is able to help her abandoned daughter feel lovable and worthy rather than rejected and guilty, to help her daughter distinguish between who her father is and what he did. If you were such a daughter, as you grew and learned more about the situation, you probably were able gradually to sort out your feelings and understand your father—even if you weren't able to forgive him.

If your dad abandoned your family, you might be asking, "But why am I so different from other daughters who grew up without their dads? Why was it so much harder for me?" Well, there are many variables. For instance, before your dad left, did you have a good relationship with him? How was your relationship with your mom? Why did your father leave? Did he stay away for a short time, a long time, forever? Were other men around to care about you and to serve as a father model? How old were you when your dad left? How did your mother handle the situation? The answers to questions such as these can give you some insight into the way you managed to adjust.

DIVORCED DADS

"I hardly know my father," says Julia. "He doesn't know me at all."

"My dad and I were closer after he moved out than we ever were when he lived with us," says Lorraine.

When we talk about "divorced dads," it sounds as if they are all the same. They aren't. Some, no longer feeling trapped in an unhappy marriage, find that their relationships to their daughters actually improve. Others are more like Julia's father. They can't slip so easily into their new role. They feel uncomfortable with their daughters. Some struggle to stay involved, but others decide it's easier just to give up and pull away.

A father may make the mistake of assuming that when his daughter is a baby, it doesn't really matter much whether or not he is around her. When she gets older, he promises himself, he'll become more involved in her life. What these fathers don't realize is that in turning away from their girls, even very young ones, they are making their daughters feel more deprived than ever.

The little girl whose father leaves home when she is in her preschool years may see her daddy's leaving as his rejection of her, as proof that she isn't worthy of love. Or she may see it as her mother's fault: "Bad Mommy drove Daddy away." If her father stays involved in her life, it's more likely that she will be able to work out her irrational fears.

By the time a girl is in grade school, she is busy learning, making friends, and exploring the world around her. She is less dependent on her parents than she used to be. But that doesn't mean she needs her dad any less. Children at this stage are acutely sensitive to the opinions of their friends. When other kids ask her such questions as, "How come your daddy doesn't live with you?" or "Why did he leave?" or "Doesn't he love you any more?" she is almost certain to feel embarrassed, defensive, and hurt. If she doesn't have much contact with her father, her pain will be even more acute.

For most girls, being a teenager means feeling uncertain, frustrated, and confused. Having to deal with emerging hormones, feeling awkward and ugly and out of step with practically everyone, searching desperately for their own identity, and struggling toward independence, teenagers need the refuge of home. They may seem self-sufficient, but teenagers need a family to give them the strength and security to hang on.

Intellectually, teenagers are much better equipped to understand and even to accept the reasons for their parents' divorce than younger children are. And yet when a father actually moves out, a teenager's whole concept of home and family is rudely shaken up. A daughter may feel abandoned by the father who acted as a cushion between her and her mother. If a father continues to stay involved with his teenager, he can provide her with some of the help and support she needs during this difficult stage of her development.

INVISIBLE DADS

An invisible father is one who, although he is still with his family, is never around. Ever heard of anyone like that? He's not really involved with the family. He's distant, all wrapped up in his own life. When it comes to the family, he's more like a bystander than a team member. Whatever time he has available, he devotes to himself, his job, his hobby, or church. What gets left out is his family.

If you had an invisible dad, you may feel very much like the daughter whose dad was gone from the home. The effect on you may also be much the same.

YOUR PERSPECTIVE

If your dad wasn't there for you when you were growing up, you probably carried a number of feelings with you into adulthood. Do you struggle with feelings of inadequacy? Do you have problems with your sense of self-worth? Do you feel that it is somehow your fault that your family broke up?

In *Always Daddy's Girl*, H. Norman Wright tells of a woman named Jean, who told him in a counseling session: "I know of a number of families where the parents didn't care for each other. But they stayed together so it wouldn't damage their kids. For those fathers, the kids were worth sticking around. But I guess I wasn't worth even that."[1]

When you consider your dad's absence from your point

of view, both the cause and the effect center on you. Yet there is another side.

YOUR DAD'S PERSPECTIVE

Take a minute to consider the situation through your father's eyes, especially if he and your mother were divorced or separated. This major disruption was a real threat to him too. Suddenly he was facing a new life burdened down with guilt and regrets from his failed marriage. Imagine how hard it must have been for him to try to meet your needs, however poorly he may have managed it, when he was drowning in his own anxieties over what the future held for him.

For many fathers, their greatest fear is that their daughters may abandon *them*. Feeling insecure, plagued by a sense of devastating loss, and driven by his own need for love and reassurance, a father separated from his family may make unfair emotional demands on his daughter. Rather than assuring her, he may turn to her for his own assurance. In his pain and loneliness, he may press too hard.

"He insisted I call him every night," Lorraine said of her father after her parents' divorce. "He wanted to talk and talk. I just couldn't handle it. I'd look for the first chance to say, 'Well, Dad, I've got to go.'"

Almost certainly, when Lorraine's father hung up the telephone, he felt more dejected and rejected than ever. *She's on the phone with her friends for hours*, he probably thought. *So how come she can't spend a little time talking to me?*

Father's Guilt

Most divorced fathers feel some guilt for the trauma their children suffer from their broken home. In an effort to escape their guilt, fathers often act in ways that end up making things worse than ever.

"My dad used to buy me things, foolish things," Lorraine recalls with a sad smile. "One time when I was about fifteen, I took a fancy to a coat with a mink collar. It was impractical and far too expensive, facts my mother quickly pointed out. Dad bought it for me anyway. It was really an inappropriate gift. I don't think I wore that coat more than half a dozen times."

"I was such a brat when I was with my dad," Kristine admits. "He would put up with anything, and I'd take all I could get. I think he was afraid to scold me."

If your dad was overly permissive or if his only contacts with you were fun-filled sprees or elaborate gifts, you might have gotten a skewed picture of fatherhood. It may also have caused a great deal of tension between you and your mother, the one who had to deal with you in real life.

Too many separated or divorced fathers have unrealistic expectations of the kind of relationship they ought to have with their daughters. They expect their daughters to support them emotionally, to love them unconditionally, and to tell them everything they're thinking and feeling. When it doesn't work out that way, dads start pointing fingers and fixing blame. Once again, it is the daughter who is caught in the middle.

"Whenever something happens, you don't know which side to go to," Lorraine recalls sadly. "If your father says something and your mother says something else, you don't know which one is right. It goes back and forth, back and forth, and you're stuck in the middle. It's a terrible place to be."

IF YOUR FATHER REMARRIES

"Dad got married right after he and mom divorced," Julia says bitterly. "I think Carly—that's his present wife—purposely pulled him away from us."

"My dad didn't get married again for several years," says Kristine. "He didn't even know the woman when he and my mom were married. But once he got together with her, things were never the same between my dad and me."

It's a rare daughter who greets her father's remarriage with peaceful acceptance. Because many fathers feel they must have their children's approval before they enter a new marriage, they tend to press too hard. But the harder they push for acceptance, the more uncooperative, negative, and cool their daughters seem to be.

If your dad remarried, it probably triggered a reawakening of your old fears of being deserted. But not all daughters react in the same way. Depending on their temperaments, they act out their responses to their dad's remarriage in different ways. You may have spoken up and loudly proclaimed how you felt. Or you may have made your feelings known in more subtle ways. However you expressed them, your feelings and opinions probably were strong.

"I was really sad about the divorce," Kristine says. "But I always believed my mom and dad would get back together again. Even though they hardly spoke to each other, I had the whole scenario worked out in my mind. Dad would drop by with an enormous bunch of beautiful flowers. Mom would be so pleased that she'd ask him to stay for supper. One thing would lead to another, and before long, I, wearing a beautiful pink ruffled dress, would be the bridesmaid in their wedding. That dream was dashed when my dad married someone else."

Many children of divorce share this fantasy. And remarriage sounds the death knell on that comforting dream. Suddenly the child has to make peace with a whole new reality.

LIVING WITH A STEPFATHER

"I didn't want my mother to remarry because I knew I'd resent having some other man trying to take my father's place," Lorraine explains. "I was certain I would never respect him. I determined never to obey him if he told me to do something I didn't want to do. I would just look at him and say, 'Who are you to boss me around?'"

"One father was bad enough," Julia says. "I knew I didn't want two."

In an interview in *The Observer*, Russian author Alexander Solzhenitsyn talked about his own hard childhood. He said, "My mother raised me in very difficult conditions. She was widowed before I was born and never remarried, mainly because she was afraid a stepfather would be too strict."

Everybody knows about stepparents. Those fearsome myths and fairy tales aren't lost on us. Without a doubt, preconceptions about stepfathers can interfere with a family's attempt to build a new life.

In our society, we may not be able to agree on what goes into making a successful stepfather, but we are pretty outspoken about some of the things he should *not* be. For instance, everyone pretty much agrees that

1. A stepfather must not be too strict with his step-daughter. Certainly he must never seem cruel to her.
2. He must not try to take the place of the girl's natural father.
3. A stepfather must not fail to provide whatever elements of parenting his stepdaughter isn't getting elsewhere.
4. He must not fail to provide her with any further elements of parenting his wife thinks the girl needs.
5. Above all, a stepfather must never, ever do anything unloving to his stepdaughter.

Can you see the problem here? Notice how these expectations—each of which sounds pretty noble in itself—conflict with each other? Stepfathering is a relationship that pits the myth of the cruel stepparent against the fantasy of the charmingly clever television sitcom instant parent.

Now let's look at reality. Stepdaughters and stepfathers usually start out strangers to one another. Mutual acceptance is a slow process that does not respond to pressure. In an effort to appease her mom, a daughter may accept her new stepfather too quickly. But once she starts to be troubled by her feelings of loyalty to her own father, she may turn against her stepfather. And stepchildren can be pretty awful. Achieving a plane of peaceful coexistence takes time and patience and many, many concessions on both sides. Like it or not, that's how it is.

It's true that the man who married your mother is not your father. But neither is he just your mother's husband. He is someone who can provide a special dimension to your life, a dimension you will find in no one else.

Your Adjustment

You say you grew up a stepdaughter and you felt miserable about it? You say you're still trying to figure out why? Don't be too hard on yourself. Actually, there are some very good reasons for your feelings. You may recognize yourself in one or more of the following:

1. You'd already lost your father. When your stepfather entered the picture, you lost your mother too. Even if you did a pretty good job of successfully accommodating your mother's new husband, his very presence meant you had to give up that special closeness that may have grown between you and your mom. Before he entered the picture, she may have talked to you. She may have confided in you. You were her main consideration, perhaps even her best friend. But when your stepfather joined the family, you suddenly found that your mother's conversation was mainly with him. Now *he* was her most important companion. *He* was her best friend.

2. You suffered the no-win situation of divided loyal-ties. So whose side were you on? I know, I know. Everyone always told you not to choose sides. But as you quickly learned, true neutrality isn't usually possible. You had a difficult puzzle to solve—how could you manage to love two fathers and offend no one?

3. You lost your position of responsibility. When your mother remarried, you may have had to give up your adult responsibilities. This might sound like a plus to some people, but you know that it also meant you lost the satisfaction those responsibilities brought you. Mother's Helper can be a very important role to a girl. It's a hard thing to have it suddenly stripped away.

4. You had to decide whether to help your mother's new marriage work or try to break it up. Like other stepdaughters, you knew full well that marriage isn't forever. You had firsthand experience. Once your mother remarried, you may have tried to push the intruder out. But you also may have harbored a terrible fear—what if you actually succeeded?

Despite all that has been said, stepdaughters and stepfathers can have a strong, positive relationship. But to reach that point takes work, patience, and compromise. A stepfather isn't the same as a real father, no matter what anyone says.

However tense and trying your time with your step-father may have been in the past, it isn't too late to make friends with him now. Talk to him. Tell him the fears you had back then—and the ones you still have. Thank him for the times he overlooked your orneriness. Recall the times he stood up for you, the times he came through for you.

A stepfather is not a bad person to have around. One who is your friend is a real treasure. He can give a whole different meaning to the word "father."

6.
God, the Father

"*Our Father who art in heaven, hallowed be thy name.*"
So begins what we know as the Lord's Prayer. It's one of
the first portions of Scripture most of us learn. It's the only
Scripture many people ever know.

God, our heavenly Father. What a wonderful concept.
What an exciting idea.

Wonderful and exciting for some of us, that is.

"I've heard about God ever since I can first remember," says Marla. " 'God is love.' 'God is merciful.' 'God is
kind.' 'God is your heavenly Father.' When I pictured God,
I didn't see an old robed man with a long flowing beard. I
saw a man five feet, eight inches tall, who weighed one
hundred seventy-two pounds, had dark brown hair graying
at the temples, and a clean-shaven face. That, you see, was
the description of my father. To me, my father *was* God.
Heavenly Father or everyday father, what's the difference?

"My father is still around popping in and out of my life.
But God? I don't believe in him any more."

Marla is not alone. For many women, the word *father*
conjures up images of male dominance or cool distancing,
perhaps indifference or ridicule, maybe even cruelty and
abuse. For others, it brings images of gentle, loving
indulgence.

I will be a Father to you,
and you will be my sons and daughters,
says the Lord Almighty.

(2 Cor. 6:18)

What is certainly intended as a wonderful and comforting promise becomes a fearful threat to some women. It all depends on a person's experience with her father.

EARTHLY FATHER, HEAVENLY FATHER

Fathering is a high calling. God intended fathers to be the spiritual leaders of their families. They are to teach, to encourage, to provide for their children. If your father filled this role in your life, you are blessed indeed. Thank God for your dad. And thank your dad.

But if your father did not fill this role, you may end up feeling empty, cheated, and angry. And those feelings color your relationship to God.

We tend to see God through the lens of our experience with our earthly father. There's real danger in that. First, we end up having a distorted picture of God. Second, this distorted picture prevents us from receiving from God the very healing we need to have stronger relationships with our dads.

What Is God Like?

The Bible gives us some indications. It tells us that God is love. It also says he is truth and justice and mercy. God is awesome, even fearsome. But he is understanding and patient too. Yet despite these hints and clues, none of us, hampered as we are with finite minds, can begin to comprehend the full and true nature of God.

We do, however, understand the word *father*.

"What is God like?" Carrie asks. After pausing to reflect she says, "Well, he is certainly loving. And of course he is giving. He wants us to be happy." Carrie pauses again, then adds emphatically, "I do believe in God, but I don't believe in hell. God is too loving and forgiving and patient and kind to send anyone to a place like that."

Carrie is the daughter of an indulgent, affectionate father. He never punished her. All she had to do was smile and call him "Papa" and tell him how much she loved him, and he was ready to forgive her for anything.

Diana sees the matter differently. "God has favorites," she says. "Some people he really loves, like Abraham and David and Billy Graham. Then there are the rest of us. You can tell who his favorites are by watching how unfair life is. Some people get all the breaks, others get all the bricks."

Diana knows all about playing favorites. Her father had a favorite child—her brother.

"I suppose God loves me," Elise concedes. "But I sure don't expect him to get involved in my life. I mean, he's way up there with all that power over the universe. Why should he care about me?"

Elise doesn't question her father's basic love for her. Yet she has no real relationship with her father. They keep each other at a distance.

"God loves me when I'm good," says Jeanette. "But when I do wrong, watch out. He punishes and chastises me by allowing trials and difficulties to come into my life. Once when I really got my mind off him, I got a terrible case of pneumonia. But I know it's all for my good. He has to teach me and train me to do right."

Jeanette's father's love is conditional. When she meets his expectations, he shows her his love. But when she breaks his rules, his punishment is swift, hard, and sure. "It's for your own good," he always told his daughter. "It's all for your own good."

"God is powerful and mighty," says Deborah with an air of certainty. "If you don't obey his every commandment, watch out. Just look at what happened to all those nations who dared to go up against the Israelites in the Old Testament."

Deborah's father was an absolute dictator. He was the boss, ever supreme over all other family members. And his temper was quick and unpredictable. Deborah knows well what it means to live under a powerful ruler who is always ready to mete out an angry "justice."

These women have a distorted, limited view of God. And we often do too.

Our job, then, is to clear the screen and begin to build a new, accurate picture of God, our Father. Once we have that clear picture, we can begin to allow God to father us, to teach, encourage, and provide for us.

Let's start with your present idea of God. How would you describe him? Probably some picture pops into your mind. Try this exercise:

1. On a sheet of paper, write out your description of God. What do you see as his greatest attributes? How do you think he deals with people, both in general and on a personal level? How do you think he deals with you as an individual?
2. Now take another sheet of paper. This time write out a short description of your father. Be sure to include what you see as his strong points and his weaknesses. What are your memories of your dad? How did he deal with you?
3. Now compare the two descriptions. How does your perceived picture of God compare with your description of your father? Do you see any similarities?

William and Kristi Gaultiere, in their book *Mistaken Identity*, quote a psychologist who says:

"No child arrives at the 'house of God' without his pet God under his arm." And for some of us the "pet God" we have tied on a leash to our hearts is not very nice, nor is it biblically accurate. This is because our negative images of

God are often rooted in our emotional hurts and the destructive patterns of relating to people that we carry with us from our past.[1]

For many of us, the model for our "pet God" was our father. Whether your experience with your father was good or bad or a combination of both, it is a mistake to base your perception of God on him. Your father is, after all, an imperfect human being.

SEEING GOD FOR WHO HE IS

How do we get beyond our misconceptions? How can we separate who our earthly dads are and who God is? How can we free ourselves to see God as he is, without seeing him through the filter of our own experiences with our dads?

The first place to look is the Bible, where we will find what he does, what he says, and what others say about him.

God Gives Good Gifts

In Matthew, Jesus asks his crowd of listeners: "Which of you, if his son asks for bread, will give him a stone? Or if he asks for a fish, will give him a snake?" Knowing that fathers instinctively want to do their best for their children, he continues, "If you, then, though you are evil, know how to give good gifts to your children, how much more will your Father in heaven give good gifts to those who ask him!" (Matt. 7:9–12).

Undoubtedly your father did the best he could for you within the framework of what he had to give, yet however you view him, his best was far from perfect. But your Father in heaven—that's a completely different matter. God the Father *does* know how to be a perfect parent. How much more will *he* give you good gifts! This promise from the mouth of Jesus should be a real encouragement to every one of us.

God Is Merciful

In the gospel of Luke, Jesus admonishes us to "Be merciful, just as your Father is merciful." (Luke 6:36) He isn't referring to your earthly father, of course. Your earthly father may have been anything but merciful. He may have been judgmental, cruel, and demanding. But your heavenly Father is merciful and gracious. A pastor once defined God's grace and mercy like this: God's grace means he loves us even though we don't deserve it; his mercy means he doesn't treat us as we deserve to be treated. As Psalm 103:10 puts it, "He does not treat us as our sins deserve."

God's mercy and grace toward us make us safe with him. We don't need to fear that he will treat us cruelly or harshly. He overlooks what we are and loves us with a pure love.

God Is Compassionate

"As a father has compassion on his children, so the Lord has compassion on those who fear him," wrote the psalmist David in Psalm 103. Your earthly father has compassion for you. He may not readily show it. His tough exterior may make him seem completely indifferent and uncaring. Yet deep down, underneath that hard exterior, he cares about you and your pain.

If your earthly father cares about you, how much more does your heavenly Father care! God knows what you are going through, and he cares. His heart is tender toward you and your concerns. He knows all about the relationship you have with your father. And he knows about the relationship you would like to have.

In your journey toward a healthier, happier relationship with your earthly father, don't neglect to talk your desires and your concerns over with your heavenly Father. Ask God, who feels so caring and compassionate toward you, for his help and guidance.

God Loves You Intimately

Not only is your heavenly Father perfect, all-knowing, all-powerful, and all-wise, but he invites you to have a truly close and intimate relationship with him. Imagine that!

Listen to what the apostle Paul writes in his letter to the Romans: "For you did not receive a spirit that makes you a slave again to fear, but you received the Spirit of sonship. And by him we cry, 'Abba, Father'" (Rom. 8:15). We can call the great God of the universe, "Abba, Father!" Do you know what "Abba" means? It was the affectionate Aramaic term for "Daddy." You can go directly to God and call him Daddy!

You may never have felt close to your earthly father. You may never have seen him as a Daddy, a person who would take you on his knee and cuddle you, comforting you if you were sad, holding you, helping you to feel secure. Well, this verse from Romans indicates that when we become Christians, the Holy Spirit inside us invites us to call God Daddy.

Jesus, the great story teller, told his disciples of a man who owned a hundred sheep. One independent-minded little fellow wandered away from the rest of the flock. "Will he [the owner] not leave the ninety-nine on the hills and go to look for the one that wandered off?" Jesus asked. "And if he finds it, I tell you the truth, he is happier about that one sheep than about the ninety-nine that did not wander off" (Matt. 18:12–13).

Then, in case his listeners missed it, Jesus comes right out and tells us the point of the story: "In the same way your Father in heaven is not willing that any of these little ones should be lost" (Matt. 18:14).

Your heavenly Father cares about you intimately. He cares enough that in your moment of need, he focuses his full attention directly on you.

God Is Perfect

Your earthly father was not and is not perfect. You not only know that, you may have strong feelings about his many imperfections. You may have suffered deeply because of his flaws and mistakes.

In Matthew 5:48 we read this admonition: "Be perfect, therefore, as your heavenly Father is perfect." God is perfect. In his mercy, in his giving, in his love, in his compassion, in his justice, God is perfect. He never makes a mistake. He never sees anything the wrong way. He never misinterprets anyone's intentions. He can't, because he is perfect.

How healing it is for me to realize that somewhere in the world, I can find a perfect father. I need that. I need the assurance that in his perfect knowledge God, my Father, knows me better than I know myself and he knows my dad better than I will ever know him. I need the assurance that in his perfect wisdom God, my Father, divinely ordained me to be my dad's daughter. I need the assurance that in his perfect love God, my Father, has accepted me as his daughter. He is perfect.

"When I Was a Child, I Thought As a Child . . ."

When you were a little girl, it was understandable that you fashioned your view of your heavenly Father after what you saw in your earthly father. But you are no longer a child. It's time to move beyond your restricting, distorted view. It's time to catch a glimpse of God the Father as he really is.

Why is it so important for us to look at the fatherhood of God? As daughters, all of us long for a perfect relationship with our dads. We long for his love, his approval, his affection, his understanding, his mercy. But the truth is, *he can't give us all those things.* We may know that in our heads, but our hearts keep looking to that relationship to fulfill those needs. Our hearts keep expecting that maybe this time will be different. And each time we look to that earthly relationship to fulfill those deep needs, we are disappointed. Our earthly dad will never be able to fill those needs.

But God can. And will. If we realize that in God we have a father who loves us purely, who always treats us fairly, who always has time for us, who always is looking out for our good, who wants the best for us, who forgives all our faults, then we are free to rely less and less on our earthly fathers to meet our needs. When we find our fulfillment first of all in our relationship as God's daughters, that takes some of the pressure off our relationship with our dads.

The more we grow in our understanding of who God our Father is, the more we can depend on him to meet our deep inner needs. But how do we move beyond *knowing* that God is perfect, loving, merciful, and compassionate to having those qualities touch our life with all their healing power?

Let me suggest that you begin a journaling Bible study. Set aside a few weeks or even a few months to focus your Bible-study time on the fatherly attributes of God, praying that God would use this time not only to strengthen your relationship with him as your Father but also to strengthen and heal your relationship with your earthly father.

Where do you start? I would suggest you start by listing your dad's qualities that most obstruct your relationship right now. Maybe it's his explosive, unpredictable nature. Maybe it's his distant, uncaring personality. Maybe it's his lack of understanding.

Once you have a list of three or four qualities, make a list of antonyms—words that mean the opposite of the words describing your dad. For instance, the opposite of *explosive* and *unpredictable* might be *gentle, kind, patient, unchanging, the same.*

Now get a Bible concordance and look for verses that use the words *gentle, kind, patient, unchanging,* or *the same.* You won't necessarily find all those words in the Bible concordance, but you will find some as a start.

Let's take the word *gentle* as an example. For those of you who haven't used a concordance before, you will find that not every use of the word *gentle* will be a reference to God. Look through the list and write down three or four verses that look as if they may apply.

In my *NIV Complete Concordance* I see three verses that may be possibilities: Matt. 11:29 and 21:5; 2 Cor. 10:1. Next, I find the verses and read them.

- Matthew 11:29 says, "Take my yoke upon you and learn of me, for I am gentle and humble in heart and you will find rest for your souls."
- Matthew 21:5 is a reference to an Old Testament prophecy: "Say to the Daughter of Zion, 'See your king comes to you, gentle and riding on a donkey, on a colt, the foal of a donkey.'"
- 2 Corinthians 10:1 says, "By the meekness and gentleness of Christ, I appeal to you. . ."

After looking at these three verses, I might pick the first two to write in my journal and study. Then I would slowly meditate on each verse, maybe spending one day on each verse. I would write in my journal any thoughts I had about the verse. One woman who did this exercise wrote this in her journal:

Matthew 11:29—"Take my yoke upon you and learn of me, for I am gentle and humble in heart and you will find rest for your souls."

What does it mean that God [Christ, here in this verse. Words about Christ also refer to God: Christ said of himself, "Anyone who has seen me has seen the Father"] is gentle and humble? It means he's not demanding, not harsh. He doesn't expect unreasonable things from me.

He asks me to take on his yoke. The word "yoke" suggests a picture of two animals joined in a wooden yoke for the purpose of carrying a load or doing some heavy work.

God offers to share my load, my burden, my heaviness, my work. He comes alongside me and does it with me. He doesn't say, "All right, this is the load I want you to carry, and it's up to you to do it alone. I know it's heavy, but that's tough. Carry it, and you'd better do it well or you'll hear from me!"

His voice is not abrasive. I hear this invitation as a kind, helpful, attractive one. He gives me a job to do but then offers to do it with me. In case I have doubts, he tells me that he is gentle and humble. I don't have to be afraid of him or the work. I can be confident.

And then, if this were not enough, he promises a wonderful thing as a result of doing what he says. He promises that in carrying this load with him, I will find rest for my soul. Rest—again, a calm, gentle, secure picture of resting my soul in God.

How does this verse change me? I've always felt that my dad expected perfection from me. He'd give me something to do, and if I didn't do it perfectly, he'd berate me, yell at me, or make me feel worthless, even though the job I had done was usually done very well by most people's standards. I ended up feeling frustrated, angry with him and myself, worthless, and incredibly burdened by his expectations. I felt alone and insecure.

This verse gives me a whole new perception of a father's expectations. God knows I have work to do and burdens to carry, but he offers himself as part of the process. I feel his companionship and that gives me joy. I also know that I can count on his help. He offers his perfect self to help me with my burdens and work. He doesn't say, "I'll help you once, but don't expect me to do all the work for you." His offer seems permanent, unconditional. It makes me feel hopeful and eager to get on with the job of carrying the load or doing the work. He gives me confidence and security. And then he promises that the end result will not be just a completed task or a carried load but *rest* for my soul. I feel myself breathing more calmly just thinking about it. This verse is such a different picture from the turmoil I would feel with my dad.

God, my Father, is gentle. He helps me, encourages me, gives me confidence, comes alongside me, promises me rest for my deepest inner needs. I love you, Father.

As you can see from this entry, the goal is not necessarily to come to a "correct interpretation" of the verse. The goal is to let the words speak to you, to let the voice of God come to you through the verse, and then to have a conversation with him. Each day's entry will be different; each person's entries will be different. But the method allows you to let the characteristics of your Father work their way into your life, where they can replace the hurt left there by your dad and your past.

If you are hesitant to try this kind of journaling meditation because you're not sure if you can find good verses, start by meditating, verse by verse, on Psalm 103:8–14, verses that speak of these attributes of God: compassion, graciousness, patience, love, and so on.

Then spend time in other verses: the parable of the Prodigal Son, which pictures God as a Father (Luke 15); verses about prayer, assuring us that our Father knows all of our needs (Matt. 6:6–8); verses that assure us of our Father's commitment to our good (Matt. 7–12); verses about the Father who comforts us in all our difficulties (2 Cor. 1:3–5); verses about the Father who will never turn his back on us (Heb. 13:5). Once you get started, you'll find many more.

God, your heavenly Father—a Father who loves you, cares deeply about all aspects of your life, comes alongside you in your struggles and joys, promises to be with you forever, gives you all you need to live a full life. Let the reality of who he is penetrate into the deep recesses of your being. Allow him to father you.

PART II.
MAKING CHANGES

7.

Changing Your Father's Effect on You

Until now, we have been working toward increasing our understanding of what has gone before. We have wrestled with the past in order to build a sounder future. For the remainder of the book we will turn our attention to making some concrete changes. The foundation has been laid. Now we are ready to start building.

- "I've gone through job after job. Somehow I just can't seem to get along with the boss."
- "I have been married three times. Each one of my husbands turned out to be either an alcoholic or an abuser. Why can't I choose a decent man?"
- "I love my children dearly. So why do I always end up driving them crazy?"

Many of the here-and-now conflicts we women have with our spouses, our bosses, our children, and our friends are in part replays of suppressed feelings stored from incidents that happened in our childhood. The unresolved conflicts we had with our fathers always seem to reappear mysteriously, following us into our adult relationships.

It would be a mistake to blame our fathers for every problem we have. Yet we must understand that our dad's influence reaches out and touches us throughout our lives.

If your father has not been forthcoming with emotional support for you, he probably won't start now. The cornerstone to lay in place right at the beginning is your resolve to *stop blaming your father for what he didn't do for you.* The second step is to determine to *give up—forever—trying to change him.*

The secret to building a friendship with your father is to *focus on changing the effect the other person has on you.*

RECOGNIZING HIS INFLUENCES

In chapter 1 we explored the many ways our dads have influenced us—for better or for worse. You may want to take a minute to review the list you made of your dad's positive and negative influences on you. What are you going to do about changing the negative effects he's had on you?

Anything that threatens your survival will naturally bring on feelings of anger and resentment. I don't mean only those elements that threaten you physically. I'm also talking about whatever it is that threatens you emotionally—whatever endangers your self-esteem, your sense of importance, your spirituality, your very identity.

Now and then, people and situations you encounter will inevitably remind you of people and events from the past. Stressful memories are going to be ignited and reactivated throughout your life. Whether or not your memories are accurate, whether or not they do justice to your father or others important to you makes very little difference. Accurate or not, they rob you of your peace of mind and your happiness in your present relationships.

Has your husband ever said something that brought your father's old insensitive pronouncements flooding back, and you immediately reacted with a defensive outburst that shocked even you? Has your boss ever ordered you to do something, and suddenly old resentments against your dad made you bristle up and lash out inappropriately? These are signs of troubled patterns left over from the past. Your father isn't even around, yet he's still affecting you in the same old hurtful ways. And, guess what—you are letting him do it.

Another painful effect that fathers can have on us daughters is in the messages he sent about love, marriage, intimacy, and sex roles.

- "My dad always used to tell me, 'If a woman loves her husband, she'll put up with anything he does,' " says Elise.
- "When you're married, your husband is the boss," Deborah states. "That's the lesson my father taught me."
- "Love him enough and he'll treat you right," says Carrie, with a knowing nod.
- "Women can control men with their tears," Aimee says. "It always worked on my dad. Mom did it, my grandmother did it, and you can be sure I do it."

SEPARATE YOURSELF

One of the important steps in changing your father's effect on you is separating yourself from him. You need to allow yourself to become a whole and healthy person. This may mean pursuing your own goals despite his protests. It may mean declining his offer of financial assistance or physical help. Or it may mean actually putting distance between the two of you, maybe even moving out of town.

Separation is a three-step process:

1. Letting go of your dad,
2. Becoming independent, and
3. Relating in a healthy way to a man in your life.

Where do you stand in this progression? Are you still at stage one, holding tightly to your dad while proclaiming loudly that you want your freedom? (You depend on him to check out your car when it has a problem, to call the gas company when you have a complaint about your bill, to fix your leaky bathroom faucet.) Are you reluctant to give up the comfortable parts of your dependency? (Always a loan available from good old dad or a few bucks to tide you over until payday.) Do you have trouble forming relationships with other men? (Daddy doesn't like the way he wears his hair.)

Married or single, if you are an adult, you need to be able to stand alone as an independent, self-sufficient person.

YOUR SENSE OF SELF-ESTEEM

Who are you? Besides being your father's daughter, how would you describe yourself? Before you can change your father's effect on you, you need to be sure you have a good image of yourself to stand on. On what do you base your sense of self? If you aren't sure, you might ask yourself the following questions:

- How do I feel about myself? Am I a worthwhile person?
- What words would I use to describe myself?
- On what do I base my sense of value as a person?

Many of us base our ideas of ourselves on false or shaky foundations. We try to stand on the faulty ground of what others think about us. Many dads unwittingly tear down their daughter's ability to value themselves. If your father looked at your report card and proclaimed, "You are either dumb or lazy," you may have ended up believing it was true. How could your dad be wrong about something like that? Then, with the idea firmly planted in your mind, you went out and proceeded to flunk math and prove him right.

Most of us have an internal critic that guides the way we feel about ourselves and how we react to others. The problem is, the opinions of this critic are based not on facts but on the judgments other people placed on us, people such as our dads. Yet this relentless critic is quick to point out that we don't measure up to the standards set for us. In *Mistaken Identity,* William and Kristi Gaultiere explain it this way: "It's your internal parent that has idealistic self-expectations for you and is quick to criticize and condemn you for not being a 'good enough Christian.' It's the cruel perpetrator of the crime of murdering your self-esteem."[1]

The only way to achieve an honest, healthy self-esteem is to begin to see yourself through God's eyes. God is the one who knows you as you really are, with all your talents, abilities, and potentials. And he loves you more than anyone ever could.

The Bible is filled to overflowing with promises to encourage you and build you up. Here are a few you might want to consider:

- "Being confident of this, that he who began a good work in you will carry it on to completion until the day of Christ Jesus" (Phil. 1:6).
- "And God is able to make all grace abound to you, so that in all things at all times, having all that you need, you will abound in every good work" (2 Cor. 9:8).
- "I can do everything through him who gives me strength" (Phil. 4:13).
- "Who shall separate us from the love of Christ? Shall trouble or hardship or persecution or famine or nakedness or danger or sword? . . . No, in all these things we are more than conquerors through him who loved us. For I am convinced that neither death nor life, neither angels or demons, neither the present or the future, nor any powers, neither height nor depth, nor anything else in all creation, will be able to separate us from the love of God that is in Christ Jesus our Lord" (Rom. 8:35–39).

Before you can effectively love those who came before you (your parents) and those who come after you (your children), you must first love yourself. Otherwise you will succeed only in bringing your frustration and anger along into your relationships—not just your relationship with your father, but also those with your friends, your co-workers, and, if you are a parent, with your own children. By first nourishing your own life, you will find the strength to meet the demands of nurturing your friendship with your father. The more your own needs are met, the happier and more fulfilled you will be. And the healthier you are emotionally, the more you can learn to accept and love your father without feeling driven to change him.

MAKING CHANGES

As you begin to move forward, it may be necessary for you to set new limits for both you and your father. If you feel you have played the role of victim too often, it may be appropriate for you to say as kindly as you can, "Please, Dad, back off!" If you have played the rescuer, you might say, "I love you, Dad, but this is your problem, and I can't take care of it for you." Be careful not to speak in anger. That will just make you feel guilty and put your father back in control. The idea is to help him to see and understand *your* needs—and that it is all right for you to *have* needs.

As you make changes, remember this life axiom: You don't have to adjust perfectly to *everything* in order to fully participate in life and relationships. You are allowed to have some idiosyncrasies and eccentricities. (Of course, so is your father.) It's all right to be short-sighted now and then, to be opinionated, to be stubborn. (The same is true for your father.) Do you see an important warning here? Take care to avoid demanding more of your dad than you do of yourself. And if you are the type of person who demands a great deal of herself, you would be wise to determine to demand *less* of him than you do of yourself.

As for me, I want to go on caring and loving for as long as I live. I want to feel compassion and empathy for the struggles of those who are older than I (I'll be there soon enough) and for those younger (how well I remember those days). But I'm also thinking more and more of what I need for my own sense of emotional life and health and growth. I have the right to spend some of my time and energy on my own concerns. I have reached that stage of life so ominously referred to as middle age, and I'm learning that this stage has special needs and challenges all its own. Each of us has the right to a certain amount of preoccupation with what we want to make of our own lives. We want the right; we already have the responsibility.

Once you let go of your desire to blame your father for the difficulties in your relationship and the problems in yourself, you will find yourself suddenly free to look forward to the challenge of loving him. Many of you will be able to move on to where you can put your arms around you father and say, "Come on, Dad, you put your arms around me too."

If you find it necessary to put some literal distance between you and your dad, please do not see this as a sign of rebellion or defiance against him. Moving away with the goal of mending and healing can be in the best interest of both of you. And certainly the distancing need not be permanent. The important thing is to allow yourself the time and distance you need to grow, the space to heal, and the time to contemplate the best way to rebuild your relationship.

If you can classify your father as "difficult"—if he is an alcoholic or abusive or emotionally disturbed or extremely controlling—the best way to change his hurtful effect on you is consciously to extricate yourself from him. When you set limits and boundaries for your father, he probably will strike back by trying to make you feel guilty. Or he may become angry and try to intimidate you, maybe even threaten you. Don't let him do it. Remember, you are the one in charge.

GIVING UP THE OLD ROLES

In a healthy family, every member can be who he or she is. Each person is free to change, to grow, and to develop. Family members respond to each other on the basis of who each one is.

It's different in unhealthy families. There other members act and react according to the role each is assigned. The script is acted out again and again until the role becomes a deeply imbedded part of the person's personality.

Do you play a role in your family drama? If you are ever to change your father's effect on you, you need to move out of that old role.

We discussed the roles of the rescuer and the victim in chapter 4. Here are some of the other common roles into which daughters find themselves locked:

The Pet. The pet is the role of a daddy's girl. She gets preferential treatment, is doted on by her overindulgent daddy, may be described by her siblings as "spoiled rotten." It sounds like a comfortable role, except that others in the family resent her and a pet doesn't reach adulthood very well prepared for real life.

The Rebel. When the family gets together, it isn't long before the rebel is in trouble. I once knew a rebel daughter who rode her motorcycle up the front steps of the church and into the sanctuary while her father was preaching the Sunday morning sermon. Most rebellious daughters don't act out that drastically, but rebels do have a penchant for doing something inflammatory, then sitting back and waiting for the explosion that is sure to follow.

The Martyr. Everyone dumps on the martyr, and she lets it happen. She volunteers for the hardest, most thankless family jobs, and she sacrifices far beyond what is called for. Hers is not a happy lot.

The Scapegoat. Whenever anything goes wrong in the family, the scapegoat gets the blame. Financial problems? It's her fault. She never could hold on to a dollar. Fights and discord between family members? She's to blame. She shouldn't say things to inflame others. What a painful role to be cast into! Yet it's a hard one to get out of, for without the scapegoat, someone else would have to bear the blame.

The Peacemaker. The peacemaker is forever giving in to everyone else in the family. Her role is to keep everyone happy and at peace. Sounds like a positive role, except that she never gets the chance to meet her own needs or desires.

Helpless Child. She is always the little girl. However old she is, she is never allowed to grow up and make her own way. She is overprotected and forever cared for. Although this is a crippling role, it is an especially hard one to move out of, for it offers definite privileges. A helpless child isn't expected to be responsible or self-sufficient. No one holds her accountable for anything.

Are you locked into a family role? You probably are if you

- get angry and upset any time you are with your father.
- suffer anxiety over any family get-together.
- suffer from a frequent sense of guilt and failure.
- overreact to men who remind you of your father.
- allow your father to continue to control you.
- live in constant bitterness and anger.

If you are to change your father's effect on you, you must first break out of your destructive role. Before you are with your family again, plan out your strategy. How are you going to act differently? (If you are a rebel, don't wear that short mini-skirt that you know will set your father off.) How will you act independently? (If you are the helpless child, what can you do to show you are taking charge of your own life?) What will you say when your father lights into you? ("I appreciate the suggestion, Dad, but I've decided that this time . . .") What are some safe topics you can switch to if the water gets too hot? ("Dad, tell me about that time you were in the army and . . .") Try to do as much anticipating as you possibly can. Arrive prepared. But don't try to do too much all at once. You need to give your family time to adjust.

EASING YOUR DAD'S CONTROL

What are your dad's ways of controlling you? In our society, money is often a means of emotional blackmail. Some fathers use the giving or withholding of money to manipulate their children's choice of a career, their selection of a husband, the lifestyle they pursue. Even more fathers use money to control their daughters' relationships with them.

As an adult, you can't be blackmailed unless you consent to it. It's important that you cut yourself loose from the monetary cords that bind you to your father. Financial independence is, after all, an important part of emotional independence.

HOW DO OTHERS DO IT?

Sometimes it's hard even to know what effect your father *should* have on you. You know it doesn't feel right the way it is, but how should it be?

Watching other daughters and dads interact and observing how they work together can be helpful. But as you watch and learn, be very careful that you don't throw other, more successful relationships into your father's face. Avoid making comparisons, especially at your father's expense.

And do give credit where credit is due. When your father does something right, when he responds positively or makes an honest attempt, let him know you appreciate his efforts and his progress.

What setting gives the best opportunity for you to relate well to your dad? Quiet walks together where you and he can talk? Watching ball games together on television and munching popcorn? Playing checkers? Helping him shop for a birthday present for your mom? Holidays and family get-togethers may not be the most relaxed time to work on your relationship to your dad. They may tend to bring out old family problems and force you both into those harmful family roles. On the other hand, for some daughters, having other people around can serve to diffuse the tensions and help them get along with their dads. Discover what works best for you and focus on that.

Once you change the negative effect your father has on you to a positive one, you will be ready to begin communicating with your father without feeling threatened. The next chapter will explore two of the hardest subjects with which you and your father will have to deal: expressing your anger and expressing your love.

8.

Expressing Anger, Expressing Love

Arlene is not a happy woman. Feeling trapped in a miserable marriage, she is habitually depressed and angry. At first Arlene was surprised when her counselor suggested that it was resentment and anger toward her father that was affecting her marriage, her emotions, and her entire life.

"But then, my father was always messing up my life when I was growing up," she says bitterly. "So why should I be surprised that he is still doing it today?"

Arlene's father didn't abuse her. He wasn't an alcoholic or a drug addict. He spent time at home with his kids, was a religious man, and took his family on a two-week vacation every summer. The problem was, he and Arlene just didn't get along.

"Whatever I said, my father would argue with me. If I liked something, he would turn up his nose at it. My friends were never good enough for him. I didn't take the right courses in school, study enough, or get the right grades. I couldn't ever tell a joke he thought was funny. To him, my interests and hobbies were a waste of time. Nothing I did was ever right." Arlene hasn't lived under her father's roof for over twenty years, yet even today his expectations and conditions fill her life.

Many women in their thirties, forties, and fifties, independent in numerous ways, continue to drive themselves crazy with their subconscious attempts to please their fathers. Others spend their entire lives trying desperately to get back at their fathers by defying them.

If you see yourself in either of these responses, it's important that you understand what you are doing to yourself. As long as you persist in either conforming to or rebelling against your father, you will continue to lead a dissatisfied and unfulfilled life.

"I love my dad," Tricia says. "But whenever I'm with him, I end up with a terrible headache." Many women share Tricia's dilemma. They want to love their fathers, but something always seems to get in the way.

Are you one of them? Do you want to learn to accept your dad for who he is, but his irritating old traits keep popping up between you? Do you truly long to be friends with your father, but you can't get over feeling that he's more like your boss than your buddy? Do you always get embroiled in the same old battles, even though you vow to get along?

Like love, anger has tremendous power. But while love heals and nurtures, anger poisons and destroys. Unfortunately, festering anger is an emotion endured by many women who are struggling to deal with the hurts of their childhood homes. Actually, most of us have mixed feelings toward our fathers. From them we get a bittersweet legacy of both anger and love.

ANGER

When you were a child, it probably wasn't safe for you to get angry with your father. You either would have gotten scolded, spanked, or sent to your room without supper. Most of us were punished for talking back to our dads. It's no wonder we learned to hold our anger and hurt inside. Yet most of us also discovered ways to strike back at those who hurt or frightened us.

Tricia had always resented her father for not being more sensitive to her needs. Yet she never saw the necessity of being sensitive to *his* needs. Even as an adult, it never occurred to Tricia to try to look deeper at what might be motivating her father's behavior. Her technique was the same as it had always been—ignore anything that bothered her and so avoid a confrontation. Wasn't that how nice girls dealt with their fathers? Yet even Tricia could see that putting up her emotional defenses was making her relationship with her father worse and worse.

"I never get angry," Tricia says. In her voice is a touch of self-righteous pride. "There is no advantage to letting yourself show anger."

Tricia is wrong. Anger in itself is a normal emotion. Simply rationalizing upsets or trying to shrug them off will only build up more tension. The important thing is that we learn to express our anger appropriately. Letting go of our feelings of rage safely and privately is an essential skill. Unless we master it, we can never hope to learn to communicate with our fathers.

When we were children, most of us found our dads to be both advisor and supporter. Sometimes his ideas were great; other times they were inappropriate. Or perhaps it was just that his timing was off. And at times he was just plain wrong.

But you are no longer a child. As an adult, you have the right to choose to accept or reject your father's advice. If you want to take it, fine. If you don't want to, that's okay too. Sure your dad may insist. He may argue and disapprove. But you still have a right to make your own decisions. If it turns out that you were right, you'll be glad you decided for yourself. If you were wrong, you can take responsibility and bear the consequences. Either way, by making the decision, you will be acting as an independent adult.

In the process of making friends with your father, expect that he may at times surprise you or be upset with you or make you angry. No one likes to be reproached, especially fathers.

When your father upsets you, you have two choices:

you can be disagreeably angry or you can be beneficially angry. Let's look at the dynamics of both kinds of anger.

Disagreeable Anger

Disagreeable anger shows itself in various ways. Some women suppress their feelings, smile sweetly, and hold tightly to their resentments until they explode. When that happens, their anger comes out in hurtful, inappropriate outbursts. Sometimes they become physically or emotionally ill from the poisoning effects of the anger they keep stuffed tightly inside themselves. Other women nurse their anger, carrying on mean, hostile conversations inside their minds. Still others lash out with cruel and bitter words at anyone who hurts or offends them.

Many people aren't able to direct their anger appropriately. Instead, they take it out on anyone who happens to be nearby—a member of their family, someone at work, the clerk at the grocery store, anyone.

How about you? When you're angry with your father, do you rant and rage, scream at the kids and kick the dog, or do you walk around in icy silence? Either way, your goal is the same—to punish your father for not meeting your needs.

The results of hostile anger are almost always negative and harmful. By attacking your father, you force him to fight back. He has to defend himself. By hiding behind your mask of cold indifference, you succeed only in adding to the conflict.

Beneficial Anger

On the other hand, anger can have beneficial effects. Instead of blaming and insulting your father, you can talk to him about your anger. You can explain to him that he has hurt you. Then you can tell him why you were hurt and what you need from him.

Let's see how this works. Suppose you tell your dad you got a promotion and a raise at work, and he responds by saying, "So how are you going to waste your money this time? Sink it into that lemon of a car you got suckered into?"

Now, you've been through this money discussion with him more times than you care to count. You feel your blood pressure beginning to rise. But instead of shooting back your usual retort, you say: "It really hurts me when you make fun of me, Dad. It makes me feel foolish, as if I can't make a decent decision about how to use my money. I want to be able to talk with you about what goes on in my life because you are important to me. Will you be happy with me about my promotion and raise? I really worked hard for it."

Do you notice something here? Beneficial anger is kind. It allows you to look your dad straight in the eye when you talk to him. Your tone of voice and your choice of words show that, although you are angry, you care about your father's feelings. It avoids personal attacks and accusations. It stays away from razor-sharp words like "never" and "always" ("You never approve of anything I do" or "You always make fun of me"). And it avoids personal attacks ("If you want to talk about stupid purchases, let's talk about that time when you . . .").

Beneficial anger is specific rather than general. It allows you to avoid lecturing or intimidating your father. It holds you back from trying to change him. When you use beneficial anger, you understand that it does no good to dredge up the past or pull in unrelated incidents. You get right to the point and you stay there.

Beneficial anger is receptive. After you have explained to your father how you feel, beneficial anger allows you to be quiet and listen to what he has to say. It keeps you from interrupting him. It lets you try to understand how he feels.

Beneficial anger recognizes that your father has a right to release his anger too. You may be quite surprised at the way in which your dad will react to your ability to see his point of view.

Letting Your Anger Out

Even knowing all this, are you still angry with your father? Even seething, perhaps? Try releasing that anger in some way other than silently steaming or blowing up at your dad. Try yelling at the top of your voice into your pillow. Or drive to a remote spot, roll up your car windows, and scream as loudly as you can. Pound a pillow or punch a punching bag. Run around the block—maybe two or three times. When I'm angry, I swim. The angrier I am, the more laps I do and the faster I go. Once I did forty-five laps in half an hour. That's really angry!

The point is to channel your anger somewhere where it will do you some good (exercising, for instance) or at least where it won't do any harm (screaming into a pillow).

FROM ANGER TO LOVE

Once you have been able to release your anger at your father, you will finally be free to express your love for him. A wise man once said: "There are more people who wish to be loved than there are willing to love." You may feel that your father automatically knows you love him. That's not necessarily so. He can't read your mind or see inside your heart.

Practice letting your dad know that you care about him by

- Telling him. Even though you may have choked on the words in the past, take a deep breath, step forward, and say: "I really love you, Dad." Then tell him how much you like having him tell you he loves you. Try sending him a note or a special card even when it's not his birthday or Father's Day. Put your feelings for him into words.

- Focusing on the good times, not the bad. Tell him about the times you most enjoyed being with him. Then ask him, "What do you remember as the happiest times we spent together?" You may be surprised at how many happy memories the two of you have.
- Stressing his virtues. Thank your father for the strengths he modeled. Recall to him some of the ways he has taught you, good things like setting goals or doing a good job. Tell him of ways he helped mold your values and form your principles.
- Getting to know your dad in a deeper, more intimate way. Go beyond the basic facts and center on his feelings and emotions. Ask such questions as: "What was the happiest (proudest, most satisfying) time of your life?" or "What is the most difficult (frightening, challenging) thing you've ever done?" or "When did you feel the saddest (most frustrated, most helpless)?"
- Talking about the two of you. You may find that underneath what you always saw as your dad's nagging disapproval of you is really a great deal of love and concern.
- Getting to know him spiritually. Ask your father about his spiritual convictions and beliefs. Ask him open-ended questions that will encourage him to share specific experiences with you ("When did you feel closest to God?" "What event most challenged your faith in the Lord?") Let your dad know he is important enough to you to rate a regular place in your prayers.

Unexpressed love between a daughter and her father is a tremendous burden to bear. Don't be afraid to be honest with your dad, but be careful to temper your honesty with kindness and love. Sure, there have been blunders, tears, mistakes, and misunderstandings. And there will surely be more. Yet the value of your potential relationship far outweighs the effort—and sometimes the pain—of exchanging your anger for love.

Grown-Up Love

Erich Fromm wrote: "Infantile love follows the principle: 'I love because I am loved.' Mature love follows the principle: 'I am loved because I love.' Immature love says: 'I love you because I need you.' Mature love says: 'I need you because I love you.'"

When you were a young girl, immature love was entirely appropriate. When you were a child, you were right to love as a child. But now you are an adult, and the time has come to put away childish things.

Have you ever noticed how most arguments you have with your father have little to do with the subject you are actually arguing about? For instance, if you are discussing whether or not you should try for a promotion at work, the promotion itself isn't the main issue. If you are debating the value of a television program, that program probably isn't the real problem. Your angry words really revolve around your age-old battle of "Which of us is right?" Or you might state it this way: "Who is in control here, anyway?" Somewhere along the way, love gets lost on the battleground.

If your behavior in each discussion is your way of proving you're right and your dad is wrong, he will feel compelled to fight back to prove that *he's* right and *you're* wrong. Or if he starts off the battle, you will find yourself inevitably sucked into feeling that you have to prove yourself.

The fact of the matter is that almost every issue has two sides. Certainly there is more than one way of looking at any problem. The key is to draw upon your foundation of shared love, to listen to each other, and to try to appreciate the other's point of view.

When you say, "This job promotion is the chance of a lifetime," he may counter with, "You're not home with your family enough the way it is." Well, both points may be true, and your dad's comment may be an expression of his loving concern for you. Certainly it is up to you to decide whether or not to pursue the promotion. If you respond with, "You can't let me get ahead, can you! You just can't stand to see me succeed!" you are plunging headlong into a tense situation that is sure to end with hurt and anger and will further bury your mutual love. But if you answer, "I know. That's one thing I really have to consider," you are at least acknowledging that he has a point.

What about those times when you are convinced he *doesn't* have a point? What if you walk into the house and the first thing he says is, "I hope you didn't *buy* that outfit. Whatever you paid for it, you got taken!" No wonder you bristle. But you can respond with a diffusing answer that will allow your love to shine through. You might say breezily, "I guess this is one of those outfits you either love or hate." Or perhaps, "Good thing I don't shop for clothes for you!" Then change the subject—preferably to something important to him: "Mom says you got tickets to the game on Saturday. Who are you going with?"

You let your anger rule when you

- Show your impatience with everything your father says.
- Keep yourself the focus of your conversations.
- Refuse to give in as a matter of principle, even when what your dad says makes sense.
- Insist that he give in to you.
- Make him feel foolish or old-fashioned or narrow-minded.

You let love control the situation when you

- Smile as you speak, look your dad in the eye, assume a caring demeanor.
- Talk to your father about things that are interesting to him.
- Look for topics on which you can agree.
- Ask him questions to help you better understand where he is coming from.
- Assume he really does care about you, your well-being, and your happiness.
- Try to keep criticism and judgments of him and his opinions out of your conversation.

But Can It Really Work?

"That's all well and good," you may say, "but you don't know my father. None of this is going to make any difference. He'll *never* change!"

You may be right that he'll never change. But you aren't right that your efforts won't make any difference. What you need to understand is that what your father does or doesn't do is not the measure of your success. Remember, *your goal is not to change your father; it's to change your relationship with him.* Your attitude can change from anger to love even if your father doesn't change one bit. It all depends on you.

Still need help? Here are some suggestions for building a loving relationship with your dad:

- Notice when your father says something helpful, insightful, or encouraging to you. Thank him for it.
- Share with your dad some of the ways he has helped prepare you for life: some of the lessons he taught you, some of the pitfalls he helped you avoid, some of the wisdom he imparted. Be willing to talk about what he has done right before you point out where he could make improvements.
- Recognize that you both need love from each other.

It feels great to be appreciated and admired. It's wonderful to have someone thank you and really mean it.

- Be willing to be the first one to show your love. If necessary, be willing to be the *only* one.
- Be pleased with your progress even if you see none in your father.

If you feel you can't love him, start by faith to love in little ways. Trust God to give you the love you can't muster in yourself.

Don't give up. Love is optimistic. Love thinks constructively as it recognizes the great possibilities in your father.

Anger is powerful, but love is more powerful still. In 1 Corinthians 13:13, after a majestic description of the attributes of love, the apostle Paul writes: "And now these three remain: faith, hope, and love. But the greatest of these is love."

Nowhere is this more true than between a daughter and her father. And what makes it possible is forgiveness. Read on to find out what role forgiveness plays in building toward your ultimate goal of friendship with your father.

9.

The Role of Forgiveness

This is certain, that a man that studieth revenge keeps his wounds green, which otherwise would heal and do well.
—Francis Bacon

"I'll never forgive my father!" Deborah exclaimed. "Not after what he has done to me. To forgive him would be to let him off too easily."

Deborah's father, an outspoken minister who was quick to pass judgment on his small flock—and anyone else, for that matter—carried on an incestuous relationship with his daughter from the time she was five years old until she confronted him and threatened to expose him when she was fourteen. If anyone had a reason to be bitter and resentful toward her father, it was Deborah. And resentful and bitter she was.

But what Deborah didn't understand was that her resentment was exacting a far more terrible toll on herself than on her father. That's what happens when anger, bitterness, and animosity are clutched tightly to oneself. It's like steadily swallowing small doses of poison.

Some women simply cannot—or will not—forgive their fathers for the pain inflicted on them in childhood. What such women fail to realize is that by clinging to their pain, they allow the one who hurt them to continue to control their lives.

"He ruined my life," Deborah says. "My entire childhood was miserable. I looked strange, acted strange, and had a strange family. My dad insisted I had to wear brown, sensible oxfords. Everyone laughed at my 'boy's shoes.' I wasn't allowed to shave the heavy, dark hair off my legs. Father said shaving would 'draw attention' to them. I wasn't allowed to wear gym shorts. Father was afraid boys would see me 'half-naked.' I can never remember being anything but odd, someone the other kids laughed at and ridiculed."

For Deborah, healing can't begin until she first arrives at the point where she can forgive her father. And though your grievances against your father may be for far less, the same is true for you. Do you have trouble trusting people? Do you feel uncomfortable with intimate relationships? Do you find it difficult to form positive friendships? Do you have trouble showing your affection for people for whom you truly care? All of these problems could be due to unresolved pain and hoarded resentments you are harboring toward your father. People who cling to their hurts often wind up alone and isolated.

It has been said, "He who cannot forgive others breaks the bridge over which he must pass himself." What a sad fate for those who have already suffered so much.

Forgiveness—God's Way

In the Lord's Prayer Jesus taught his disciples to pray, "Forgive us our debts, as we also have forgiven our debtors" (Matt. 6:12). But Jesus' words don't end there. He goes on to say, "For if you forgive men when they sin against you, your heavenly Father will also forgive you. But if you do not forgive men their sins, your Father will not forgive your sins" (Matt. 6:14–15).

God is a forgiving Father. This is made clear throughout Scripture. In Psalm 86:5 we read, "You are forgiving and good, O Lord, abounding in love to all who call to you."

And it is God who set the model of forgiveness for us.

He established the standard. The apostle Paul wrote, "Be kind and compassionate to one another, forgiving each other, just as in Christ God forgave you" (Eph. 4:32).

This is not just a pie-in-the-sky ideal. No, it's an ideal toward which we are to strive earnestly. In Mark 11:25 Jesus tells us, "And when you stand praying, if you hold anything against anyone, forgive him, so that your Father in heaven may forgive you your sins."

What Is Forgiveness?

What is really involved in forgiveness? I don't mean God's forgiveness. God can forgive us and remember our sin no more. He can remove our transgression from us as far as the east is from the west (Ps. 103). But we are not God.

We live with a lot of myths about forgiveness:

- "Forgiveness erases the pain."
- "If you forgive, it's as if the transgression never happened."
- "If you truly forgive, you will also forget."

Here's how Jesus taught his disciples about forgiveness (Matt. 18). Peter asked him, "Lord, how many times shall I forgive my brother when he sins against me? Up to seven times?"

Jesus answered, "I tell you, not seven times, but seventy times seven."

Then Jesus told a story about a king who wanted to settle his accounts with his servants. One poor servant owed him ten thousand dollars. There was no way he could pay that amount.

When the king saw he wasn't going to get his money, he ordered that the debtor, along with his wife, children, and everything they owned, be sold to pay the debt. When the servant heard the sentence, he fell to his knees before the king. "Please, please," he begged, "be patient with me and I will pay you back everything!"

When the king saw the poor man's despair, he took pity on him. The king canceled the debt and let his servant go free.

Too bad the story doesn't end there.

When the servant went out from his master, he immediately hunted up a fellow servant who owed *him* a hundred dollars. The servant grabbed his debtor by the throat and started choking him. "Pay me back what you owe me!" he demanded. "Pay me right now!"

His debtor fell to his knees and begged, "Please, please be patient with me and I will pay you back!"

But the first servant flatly refused. Instead, he insisted that the man be thrown into prison until every single penny was paid back. No arguments, no discussion, case closed.

Now, the other servants saw everything that happened. Boiling mad, they hurried off to tell their master, the king, all about it.

When the king heard the story, he immediately called back the first servant. "You wicked servant!" he roared. "I canceled all that debt of yours because you begged me to. Shouldn't you have had mercy on your fellow servant just as I had on you?"

The king was furious and turned the servant over to the jailer to be tortured until he paid back every last cent of his debt.

Jesus told his listeners, "This is how my heavenly Father will treat each of you unless you forgive your brother from your heart."

The message is clear: forgive your brother—forgive your father.

What do you have to forgive your dad for? Neglecting you? Humiliating you? Harming you physically? Causing you mental distress? Your pain may be tremendous. Your father's trespasses against you may be so great that the scars will be with you for life.

Ah, but wait a minute. What is the extent of the forgiveness God has extended to you? Think about it: God has willingly and lovingly bridged the gap between you and himself. His forgiveness for you has absolutely no limit. It can't be measured. It has no boundaries, no end point. However great your father's indebtedness to you, it can't begin to compare with your indebtedness to your heavenly Father.

How, then, are you to forgive? Colossians 3:13 tells you how: "Bear with each other and forgive whatever grievances you may have against one another. Forgive as the Lord forgave you."

What a big order! And it isn't just a suggestion, either. It's a command. That's the what. Now the big question: How?

HOW CAN I FORGIVE MY FATHER?

I won't kid you. It isn't easy to forgive. But God doesn't command us to do anything we are not capable of doing. Forgiveness *is* possible. Yes, even between you and your dad.

It's Your Decision

Your first step is to decide that you are willing to let go of your anger and resentments and to give up your desire for revenge. By making the choice to work through your feelings and to allow them to be replaced by forgiveness, you will be freeing yourself to live again. To agree to forgive your father will allow you to change your relationship with him from one of resentment and anger to one of love. You may still disagree with each other. That's all right. You may even express your feelings of anger or hurt, as long you do it with an attitude that will keep you from feeling alienated from him. You may even find that you will learn something from him!

Recall Specifics

Once you've made the decision to forgive your father, you are ready to begin to work through your feelings toward him. It works best to get out a pencil and paper and actually write down your thoughts as if you were directing them to your dad.

What do you resent most about your father? I mean, specifically. Instead of, "You made my childhood miserable," you might list such statements as

- I was humiliated when you spanked me in front of my friends at our Christmas party when I was eight years old.
- I resent you for getting drunk instead of taking me out on my seventh birthday.
- I resent that you used to punish me without ever giving me a chance to explain myself.

Don't worry about trying to remember every last thing your father ever did. If you have filled up a page, you have written enough.

Please understand: This list *is not* for your father to see. And it's not to help you call up all your old grievances so that you can better punish him. The list is for you and you alone, to help you focus on your specific resentments for the purpose of working through them. As you remember incidents, expect to feel sad and angry and hurt. But under no circumstances should you show your list to your father. It is not intended as ammunition. To use it as such will just increase the hostility and widen the chasm between you.

When you were growing up, you probably couldn't speak up for yourself. Now is the time to change that. Using your list of grievances as a guide, write a letter to your father. Write it out as if you were actually going to give it to him (although you won't). Write to him about those things that hurt you. Tell him what you missed in your childhood, what you wish had happened, what type of relationship you are now hoping for, what you most want from him.

Again, it's very important that you *not* show this letter to your father—or to your mother, either, for that matter, or to anyone else. It's merely a tool for you, to help you to get the anger and resentment out of your system. It may surprise you to discover how deep your pain and hurt go. This is your chance to let it all out. The time to approach your father will come later. This is the time to work on you.

After writing out her list of resentments, Deborah wrote a working letter to her father. It started this way:

> Dear Dad,
>
> For the first time in my life I'm daring to tell you how I feel about the pain and humiliation you caused me when I was growing up.
>
> One thing that really hurt me was when you hired Joseph [her brother] to spy on me at school. I knew you paid him to tell you if I rolled up my skirts or put on lipstick or wore nylon stockings. I felt betrayed and distrusted.
>
> Dad, you always told me the sexual advances you made on me were a way of showing me your love. That was a lie. You used me, and in doing that, you destroyed my ability to trust anyone who says he loves me. That is the thing about you I find hardest to forgive.

Deborah's letter went on for several pages. In it she poured out her hurts, resentments, and anger. This is the way she ended it:

> I know you are sick with cancer, Dad. Mom tells me the doctor says your chances of survival aren't very good. I really don't want you to die with me feeling the way I do about you. I still don't trust you, and I would never allow you to be alone with my children. But I do want to love you, and I do forgive you. I've been hurting for too long. Maybe you have too.
>
> Your daughter,
> Deborah

"I thought writing this letter for no one but me to read would be a waste of time," Deborah admits. "But I was wrong. I sat there and read it again and again, and each time I read it, I cried more. Then I began to realize the choice before me. I could keep on harboring my anger and building my resentment higher and higher, or I could try to understand my father and move toward him. I decided I wanted to know my father. For the first time in my life, I was willing to consider forgiveness as an option."

Talk to Your Dad

Have you finished writing out your letter? Good. Read it over as many times as you feel necessary. When you are finished reading, throw it away. Destroy your list of grievances too. Both have served their purpose. The preparation is done, and you are ready to talk to your dad.

Set up a time when you can be together for some uninterrupted time, in a setting that is relaxed and non-threatening for both of you. Rather than jumping right in with your pain and hurt, however, start out explaining to your father what you would like your relationship to be. You might say, "Dad, I want to be your friend. I want to be able to tell you the things that are important to me, and I want to know about the things that are important to you." Then you might proceed to tell him something specific about yourself, something nonthreatening. ("Did you know I'm taking a wood carving class?") Or you might reminisce about a special event that involved the two of you. ("I'll never forget that time you took me to the circus. It was so much fun! Remember when you bought that cotton candy. . . .") Even if your dad didn't do much with you, you will surely be able to remember some good times. ("I remember the day Mom took me to your office and you let me sit in your chair. I was so proud to be your daughter!")

Now ask your father about his recollections. What is his happiest memory of you and him together? What is his favorite picture of the two of you? What is his best vacation memory about you?

Your goal is to begin to talk to your father and to share with him in a positive, nonthreatening, nonconfrontational way. It won't all happen at once. Your first times of sharing may be very short. But as you begin to talk, you will also begin to communicate. As you communicate, you will find yourselves moving closer together. As you come together, you may discover that forgiving the past is not so impossible after all.

Now Is the Time

The season for forgiveness is now. Be careful that you don't fall into the trap of waiting for a time that may never come. You might be saying, "If only my father would stop drinking (tell me he's sorry, say he loves me, apologize to me), then I could forgive him." Sure, his alcoholism or his stubbornness or his indifference or his past abuses and broken trusts can make forgiveness difficult. Yet whatever your circumstances, you *can* take the first steps, and you can do it now.

Easy? Not at all. In fact, it may be the hardest step you'll ever have to take. Ask God for strength. Ask him for wisdom and discernment. You may want to begin by thanking God for the unmeasurable forgiveness he has afforded you.

Only forgiving people are truly able to understand forgiveness. When you take those first few steps, you will see that forgiveness comes by doing. Once you begin to forgive your father, you will be ready for the next step—acceptance.

10.

Accepting Your Dad for Who He Is

When I was young, I decided Rex Morgan, M.D. would be the ideal father for me. He was handsome, wise, and he always did the right thing and made the right decision. Of course, he was just a character in the comic strips, but I was sure there was a real Rex Morgan, M.D. out there somewhere, and I longed to be his daughter (that is, if he ever gave in and married his nurse, June Gale).

Comic-strip dads and television dads have it easy. They don't wake up in the morning with their hair sticking up. They don't come home from work in grouchy moods. They get time to plan out their actions and their words, and they never have to look back wishing they had reacted differently—unless it's all part of the story, of course.

Not so with real-life, twenty-four-hours-a-day dads.

"My mom and dad loved each other so much," Tricia says. "I always wanted to have a marriage like theirs. Then, five years ago, Mom learned she had liver cancer. Within months she was dead. We were all shocked and sad. Dad was devastated.

"A few months later, while settling his and my mother's business affairs, my dad made friends with a sympathetic bank employee. Two months after that, he married her.

"I can no longer accept my father," Tricia says

bitterly. "Not with that new wife of his. Not after the way he betrayed my poor mother."

Diana's story is different. "My father is an embarrassment to me," says Diana. "He is fat and sloppy, he is narrow-minded and opinionated, and he has no interest greater than what's for dinner and what's on television. The two of us have nothing in common. I do love him, and I have forgiven him for the past, but accept him? I don't know if I can."

Your dad may be exactly what you want him to be. Or he may be exactly the opposite. Most likely, he falls somewhere in between these two extremes. But whatever your father's attributes or failings, remember: you are not likely to change him. You need to accept him the way he is. Until you are able to do this, you will be unable to move forward in making friends with your dad.

ACCEPTING VS. IMPROVING

Arlene's pattern with her dad was one of emotional warfare. Arlene would sulk and blame and pull back any feelings of affection for her father. He, in turn, would criticize her, then act like a martyr when she would bristle and react. Each one felt it was totally the other person's fault.

Blaming, complaining, and insisting that your father change, places you in the middle of a no-win situation. It won't work. What it will do is make both of you more frustrated and angry, and in the end you will feel more guilty and resentful than ever. The more you put your father in the wrong, the more he will have to defend himself and prove to you that he's right. And the angrier you allow yourself to become at him, the more his irritating traits will annoy you.

The paradox is that if you want your dad's attitude toward you to change and if you want a different quality of relationship with him, you have to first accept him the way he is.

EFFECTIVE COMMUNICATION

Acceptance starts with effective communication, a skill many fathers and daughters have never learned.

How did your dad communicate with you when you were growing up? Did the two of you talk a lot, occasionally, or rarely? Did your father have trouble expressing himself but show you by his actions how he felt? Could you get through to each other or might you just as well have been on different planets? Was he affirming to you or mainly critical? Did he share feelings with you or just facts? Do you feel the two of you were able to really understand each other?

In the minds of many women, one major problem with men is that they have trouble communicating, especially where their feelings are concerned. While women often strive for a sharing of emotions, many men find it extremely difficult to do more than simply share information. But talking is just one part of communication—and often the least important part at that.

Responsive Listening

A powerful communication tool is what I call responsive listening, which involves three steps:

1. Listening from your dad's perspective,
2. Admitting that you're not always right, and
3. Keeping your temper and patience intact throughout the exchange.

That doesn't sound too hard, does it?

Listen from Your Dad's Perspective

The challenge here is to try to put yourself in your dad's shoes. Consider his parents, his environment, the values he was raised with, the way his parents related to him.

Let's say you come home from work and sink into a chair, sighing that you're tired, yet you still have a list of things to do. Your dad starts in with his old line: "I don't know why you have to work, anyway. Why, in my day a woman stayed home and raised the kids and kept the house clean for her family and. . . ."

Instead of jumping in with an exasperated, "You're so hopelessly out of touch, I may as well be talking to a brick wall," look at the situation from his perspective. Instead of blaming and attacking your father for his opinions, try looking for the reasons behind them. What experiences worked together to form them? Where did your dad's underlying attitudes come from? If you listen to him and do your best to look through his eyes, you just may discover that if you had been raised as he was, in his time and in his environment and with his values, you just might hold the same opinions yourself.

What your dad says makes perfect sense to him. Instead of fighting back, you might answer, "Sometimes I wish I could do that, but it's not an option for me if we're going to make the house payments."

Receptive listening is listening without judging or criticizing. Would you criticize your dad for saying, "I don't like liver and onions"? Surely not. When you come to where you can see an issue from his point of view, you will be just as unlikely to criticize him for responding to your weariness by saying, "A woman's place is in the home."

Ask yourself: "When I listen to my dad, can I honestly say, 'I do understand what you're saying' or 'I see how you can feel that way'?"

I know, I know. You're probably thinking that you can't agree with all the things your father says.

You don't have to agree with them. Your father is not the one in charge of your life. You have every right to think your own thoughts and to form your own opinions. But consider this: We all need and deserve both respect and the right to express our feelings. If your dad knows you understand him—or that you are doing your best to understand—and that you do appreciate his point of view, he will be much more likely to do his best to work with you rather than against you. The more you accept him as a worthwhile person, the less your differences will lead you into arguments and hard feelings. And the more you understand and accept your father, the more likely he is to understand and accept you.

You may never come to the place where you can honestly say, "I understand how you feel." But you can say, "I appreciate how you feel," and then let it go.

Admit You're Not Always Right

In your mind, the real problem is that your dad thinks *he's* always right. That attitude makes this step especially hard for you. But the fact is that in many situations there is no right and wrong, just different ways of seeing things.

If you are willing to concede to your father that you aren't always right, maybe he will be able to do the same. Just imagine how many arguments such an approach would prevent, arguments no one is going to win anyway.

When your father expresses an opinion you can't agree with, try responding with something like, "I'm glad you told me that, Dad," or "I appreciate knowing how you feel about it," or "I can see you feel strongly about this. You've obviously given it a lot of thought." Affirmation without agreement. A nice compromise, don't you think?

Keep Your Temper and Your Patience Intact

You may be used to arguing with your dad or yelling at him or stomping off when he says something you think is "stupid." Since those tactics have obviously not proven to be good relationship builders, try a new approach. Keep your irritation in check and try to look for the truth and reason in what your father says.

And as you listen to your dad, practice throwing in a few relationship-building comments like "I love you" and "I care" and "thank you." You can say it to him even if he doesn't say it to you.

Start Slow and Easy

As you begin to develop a new communication style with your father, start slowly. Talk to him about things that are both interesting and nonthreatening to him. A good way to start is to talk about him. You might ask questions like these:

- What special memories do you have about your childhood? What was it like to grow up on a farm?
- What were your parents like? How did you get along with them? Do you think they treated you fairly?
- To which brother or sister were you closest? Which did you get along with least well? What do you think made the difference?
- In what ways am I most like you?
- In what ways am I least like you?
- What quality that you learned from your parents would you want me to learn from you?
- For what would you most like to be remembered?

It was questions like these that got my dad and me started on our day-long talking spree. He told me about how he left Missouri and rode the Greyhound bus to San Francisco, full of hopes for a better life for his family. He told about his father's rule that he was in charge of his trouble-maker younger brother, and that if Herb got into trouble, my dad would be punished. We compared notes on the "internal alarm systems" we both have that make alarm clocks unnecessary for us. We talked about our mutual love for chocolate. He told me how he wished he'd been able to go to college as I had done.

Once he started, my father, who usually answers questions in single syllables, talked and talked and talked. What a wonderful day it was!

Be Attentive

Researchers who study the rhythms of conversation recognize the importance of taking turns when we talk. The proper rhythm of conversation involves both getting and giving attention. The magic of sometimes being a silent, attentive listener is that the speaker gets a chance at your attention. And if the listener is also attentive, it shows. The speaker, in turn, relaxes and feels warmer toward his listener, more inclined to take his turn at giving attention.

Whenever you are angry or anxious and find yourself wanting to break in on your dad, take a sip of water or consciously fold your hands and smile. You may find that such simple steps can help you stay in control of the situation.

In the past, psychologists advised us to be quick to "talk things out." But in dealing with your dad, your greater struggle may be to remain silent and tolerant.

When You Have to Speak Up

"Sometimes it's useless to try to talk to my father," you might be saying. When such a time comes, try using a strategy that we too often overlook—waiting. Sometimes it's a wonder what a small dose of determined silence can do.

Certainly there are times when it is important *not* to keep our mouths shut—to counter blatant injustice, for instance, or to soothe a hurt or to straighten out a misunderstanding. At such moments, we are obligated to speak out. Here our task is to find the words that are at once the most helpful and the least abrasive. Yet even when we must speak up, a moment's reflection can make what we have to say more precise, more well couched in love, and more effective.

A friend told me about her father's habit of telling insulting ethnic jokes. "He would always greet me with, 'Have you heard the one about . . . ?' and launch into one of his embarrassing put-downs."

For years my friend said nothing. Finally, one day after a particularly offensive story, she decided to speak up. "I know that to you it's just a joke," she told her father in as kind a way as she could. "But I have friends of many different national backgrounds. To me, telling jokes at their expense isn't funny, and hearing you tell them makes me very uncomfortable."

Her dad was genuinely surprised. But he took her words to heart. Never again has my friend heard her father tell such a joke.

My friend was wise. She carefully considered her words and their effect, then she spoke honestly and forthrightly, yet with kindness, being careful not to accuse or condemn.

Here's a good rule to help you decide whether to speak or to hold your peace: Ask yourself, "Will what I am going to say improve either the situation or our relationship?" If the answer is no, keep quiet. If you can honestly answer yes to one or both, take time to consider your words, whisper a prayer for wisdom and discernment, then speak up in loving kindness.

Down the Line

Once the lines of communication have been successfully opened between you and your dad, you will want to move on to discuss tougher issues. You can get ready for that time by giving consideration to such questions as

- What issues have you and your father never discussed or settled?
- Which of these would you like to discuss with him?
- What might change if you were to talk about these?
- How will you handle it if your dad doesn't respond positively to your sharing?

When you talk with your dad, remember that the point is to achieve healing between you, not to punish him or cause him pain or force him to change.

Take the Risk

"For a long, long time I have loved my dad in a desperate way," Aimee says. "I was an only child, and my mother died suddenly when I was a teenager. I always resented my dad for the way he deserted me emotionally just when I needed him most. Within months of my mother's death he was dating, and soon he was remarried. His new wife didn't care about me at all. Over the years my anger toward my father has grown, but the funny thing is, I have also felt more and more drawn to him. Finally I took the risk and told him that I had forgiven him. When I did, a funny thing happened. My father smiled and hugged me tight and said, 'I forgive you too!' "

What Aimee had not realized throughout her long years of resentment was that her father had resentments of his own. When they talked about it, he told her, "That was the hardest time of my life too. I had no experience at being a mother." Why had he gotten involved with another woman so quickly? "Because I was convinced you needed a mother. It was a big mistake, but at the time I thought it was the right thing to do." Then, with tears in his eyes, he added, "My second greatest hurt was seeing how terribly unhappy I had made you."

"Just imagine!" Aimee says. "All those years I was angry at my father for something he had done for me."

Now and then a woman will find that her father wants no part in her move toward a better father-daughter relationship. If, after you have changed your role, your father is still inflexibly fixed in his, he may no longer be able to relate to you. On the other hand, even though he himself refuses to change, he may grant you a grudging respect.

Yes, accepting your father as he is, with no promise of a change on his part, is risky. But then consider your alternative. Without that acceptance, you will never be able to gain the kind of friendship we will be discussing in the next chapter.

11.
Your Father, Your Friend

Your father is a lucky man. You've gone through a great deal of work to cement a sound relationship with him. Some parts have been pretty tough. But through it you've come to understand your dad, and you've changed his effect on you. You've forgiven him, and you're practicing communicating with him. You've even gone so far as to accept him just as he is, no strings attached. Come along one step farther. Now it's time to make friends.

THE QUESTION OF CONTROL

We have talked about achieving independence from your father. Are there still some dependence weeds that are interfering with the full blossoming of your friendship? If you aren't sure, ask yourself the following questions:

Is my father's influence on my life appropriate to my age and status? Charlotte has owned and managed her own tailoring business most of her adult life. Yet her dad continued to come over to help out with the books. Charlotte says, "My books were in fine shape. Yet my father always came up with some 'better way' to do something. He insisted that without him I'd be out of business tomorrow. When we finally began to communicate, I was able to explain how this made me feel. Now he waits for me to ask for his help."

Does my dad seem to need to check up on me? Thirty-seven-year-old Marla had lived on her own since she was twenty-two. Yet her father constantly called to see if she needed help with anything, if her car was running all right, if she was out of money. "He didn't do this to any of my sisters," Marla says. "Just because I wasn't married he thought I couldn't make it without him. When I finally told him that his checking up really bothered me, he pulled back a little. But the real change came within myself. As I listened to him, I began to understand that he was acting out of true loving concern for me. I am learning to accept his calls in the spirit in which he is giving them."

Does his desire to see me and talk to me seem to be the result of guilt or need rather than the sole enjoyment of being with me or hearing my voice? If your dad's constant intrusion on your life is a problem for you, you might try setting aside a scheduled time to be with him or to talk with him on the telephone. You might tell him something such as, "I appreciate your wanting to be with me, Dad, but I have other plans today. Let's do something together on Saturday afternoon," or "I will call you on Thursday nights at eight o'clock. That will be our time to talk."

Does he understand if I tell him that I need more space, or does he get depressed and hurt? "When, after forty years of marriage, my mother and father were going through a time of estrangement, my dad just about smothered me with his presence," Jeanette says. "He was at my house all the time." Although Jeanette understood and felt for her father's problems, she found herself resenting him more and more. When she tried to talk to him, he first became defensive, then depressed. "The changes began when I stopped doing all the talking and started to do more listening," Jeanette says. "He was really hurting!" If you talk to your father with love and gentleness, and if you listen to what he has to say, you should be able to establish independence for yourself without causing him to feel threatened.

Am I still financially dependent on my father? If you intend to be the one to set the course for your relationship with your father, you will find it's almost impossible to do so if he is still involved in your financial support. That is a parent-child relationship, not an adult-adult one. If you keep yourself in the child role, don't be surprised to find that your father doesn't treat you like an adult. "The financial help he gave me was nice," Aimee says, "but our new adult friendship is far better."

Does my father have friends of his own, or does he look to me to provide him with his only companionship? Despite all you and your father have in common—and there may be a great deal—you and he need your own circles of friends. If he insists, "You're my best friend," or "I don't need anyone else, I've got you," do all you can to help him build up his own independent friendships. "It was a major breakthrough when Dad started having lunch at the senior center," Jeanette says. "Suddenly he had someone besides me to talk to. And he quickly learned he was not the only one with problems. Now he goes over there every day to eat and visit and play checkers."

Does my father accept the fact that my commitments to my husband and children come before my commitment to him? "He expected me to drop everything and run to him when he called," Daryl says. "One day he telephoned to say he needed me. I told him my daughter had a big basketball game and I wanted to be there to watch her play. When he insisted I come anyway, I got worried and went to him. His big problem was that his television set wasn't working right." It's normal and right to want to go to your father when he really needs you. You would do that for any dear friend. But do remember your priorities.

An honest appraisal of questions such as these will help you to clear away the last of the remnants of dependency and control.

Find Solutions That Work for Both of You

Being friends doesn't mean there will be no more problems. But from now on, when a problem does arise, it will no longer be a question of which of you is going to win and which is going to lose. Whatever the problem, if you work on it, you will probably be able to come up with a solution that will satisfy both your dad's needs and your own.

When Charlotte met Ben in high school, she liked him right away. They dated some their senior year, then saw more and more of each other after graduation. "He's so great," Charlotte remembers telling her parents. "He is kind and thoughtful and caring." When she was away at college and Ben was attending an electronics technical school near their hometown, Charlotte told her parents, "He writes me the sweetest letters. He has the heart of a poet."

Charlotte's father was not impressed. He had high hopes for his firstborn child—certainly college, maybe law school or medical school.

"My father wanted me to marry an intellectual," Charlotte says. "That wasn't Ben. I was convinced Dad didn't care at all about my happiness. His concern wasn't for the character or the personality of a man. It was for the guy's intellectual accomplishments. Everyone else thought Ben was the greatest, but my dad couldn't stand him."

During every year of her marriage to Ben, Charlotte's father regularly reminded his daughter that her husband was not good enough for her—not smart enough, not sophisticated enough, not ambitious enough.

"Dad always wanted to be part of my life," Charlotte says, "yet he never wanted any part of Ben. On our tenth anniversary I was so excited about the pocket watch I got Ben, I ran over to my dad's house to share it with him just as I had always done in the old days. Dad just looked at the watch and grunted. Then he said, 'I saw David's report card. It was real good. The boy takes after you.'"

After fifteen years, Charlotte and Ben split up. "Ben finally got fed up with my dad's meddling put-downs," Charlotte says sadly. "And me, well, I guess I finally decided even my marriage wasn't worth putting up with my dad's never-ending badgering."

Who was right about Ben—Charlotte or her father? It doesn't really matter which of the two was right. The point is, the choice of a husband was up to Charlotte. Certainly her dad had the right, perhaps even the obligation, to talk to her about his misgivings and the reasons for them. But in the end it was Charlotte's decision.

"If I had it to do over again," Charlotte says, "I would stick it out with Ben and set distinct boundaries for my father. In fact, just last week I told my father so. I was shocked when he told me he wished I had, that we would all have been better off."

THE TIMES THEY ARE A'CHANGING

Most of our fathers grew up in an era when divorce was the sign of real depravity. Today it's a common part of life, even within the Christian community. Many of our fathers were raised in small communities, surrounded by relatives and long-time friends whom they saw at Sunday dinners and certainly every holiday, birthday, and anniversary. Today families are mobile. I have a cousin in New York I have never seen and perhaps never will. When I was growing up, my mother mainly stayed at home; she didn't even drive. Today when my dad telephones me, he usually gets my answering machine. He has trouble finding me at home. Our dads look at our lives and think, *She'd be happier and better off if she went back to the old way of doing things: the right way!*

Even with a mended relationship, there will be times when you and your dad will be out of step with each other.

When you disagree, whose way should it go? Who wins out? Does there have to be a loser?

And the Best Answer Is . . .

Your father is your friend. He really does care about you. Sure, he may continue to make unreasonable demands on you, but then are you always so reasonable yourself?

1. Move to where you can listen to your father's advice and appreciate the spirit in which it is offered without feeling you have to comply. You don't have to comply, you know. You can learn to say no in a loving way. Doing so will allow you to enjoy saying yes when you can. Being friends with your father means you can joyfully include him in your life—on your own terms.

2. Demonstrate your love creatively. "For the first time in years, I didn't dread the approach of Father's Day," Charlotte says happily. "Instead of searching the racks for an innocuous, noncommittal card, I made a card of my own. Actually, it turned out to be more like a booklet because I included pictures of some of my favorite times with my father. On each page I wrote out the things I remember him doing that meant a lot to me and showed me his love. For instance, I wrote, 'Thank you for always sticking up for me when Mom got on my case' and 'Thanks for taking me fishing instead of telling me girls don't do things like that' and 'Thank you for believing me and standing up for me when I was accused of cheating in high school Spanish.' I ended it with, 'I'm so lucky to have a dad who really cares about me.' And you know what? I really meant it!"

3. Remember to see things from your dad's point of view. Today's new fathers, the ones who are just learning how to change diapers and warm bottles at midnight, understand the importance of expressing love to their daughters a lot better than did men of our fathers' generation. It was harder for our dads back then, and it's still hard for many of them today. Rejoice with him for how far he has come.

HOW FAR ARE YOU WILLING TO TAKE YOUR FRIENDSHIP?

Carol Flax and Earl Ubell, in their book *Mother, Father, You*, describe four levels of relationships daughters can have with their fathers[1]:

1. Minimal relationship. At this level, daughters and fathers talk, but that's about it. The main goal is to speak to each other and not fight. There is great emotional distance between the two. It's a shallow relationship, yet it can serve as a stepping stone to a deeper one.

SAMPLE CONVERSATION:

Daughter: Why didn't you tell me Aunt Ida was getting married?
Father: I figured you wouldn't care.
Daughter: I might want to go to the wedding.
Father: Do you?
Daughter: I don't know. But I'd at least like to have the option.
Father: So you have the option. Do you want to go?
Daughter: I don't know. I didn't know anything about it until now.

2. Moderate relationship. In this relationship the father and daughter want want more than just talk. They want mutual emotional support. They are willing to give it if it's needed and to accept it if the other offers. There is also a greater degree of listening to each other's needs and hurts than in a minimal relationship. There is a nurturing feeling between them. To be involved at this level, you may have to do more giving than taking.

SAMPLE CONVERSATION:

Father: I was just calling because I was lonely.
Daughter: Okay. Let's talk.
Father: Did I tell you Aunt Ida is getting married?
Daughter: No. Are you going?
Father: Of course, she's my sister. And I'll have a chance to see some old friends.
Daughter: That's great, Dad. You'll have a nice time.

3. *Strong relationship.* This is definitely a mutually helpful relationship. Each side is willing to help the other if needed and willing to accept help if it is offered. The difference is that the help is more than emotional help. This relationship involves a willingness to *do* something.

SAMPLE CONVERSATION:

Father: Aunt Ida's getting married.
Daughter: Really? When?
Father: Next weekend.
Daughter: Are you going?
Father: I wish I could, but it's too far for me to drive.
Daughter: Why don't I drive you? It will be fun to see the relatives.
Father: You have a busy life. I can't let you take your whole weekend to drive me up there.
Daughter: I'll be happy to take you, Dad. I know how much it means to you.

4. *Ultimate relationship.* This strongest of relationships is actually a combination of all three preceding it. This is truly a trusting, loving relationship where both father and daughter are free to reveal their inner needs, thoughts, and

feelings. Each wants to offer safety to the other. Each wants to give and receive comfort. This level does not come easily or quickly. It should be the goal of every father-daughter relationship, even though it isn't always an attainable goal.

SAMPLE CONVERSATION:

Father: Aunt Ida's getting married next weekend.
Daughter: How wonderful! Let's make a weekend of it and drive up there.
Father: I don't know. You have a pretty busy life.
Daughter: It will give us a wonderful chance to talk and do some things together, just you and me. I can't wait.

On which relationship level are you and your father? Certainly you are at least at the level of a minimal relationship. Very few of us have achieved a consistent level of the ultimate relationship. Wherever you are, take your father by the hand and start climbing. For the two of you, the sky's the limit!

NOW IS THE MOMENT

"When I was in my twenties, I thought I was too angry at my dad to ever be friends with him," Evelyn said. "In my thirties I was too busy resenting him, blaming him for everything that was wrong in my life. In my forties I finally began to look at him differently, but I wanted him to come to me on my terms. Last year my father had a heart attack. I was terrified that I had waited too long, that I never would get to know him as a friend. Fortunately, he survived. I got one more chance, and I made friends with my father. How I wish I hadn't waited so long!"

You and your dad have come a long way. Although you never want to quit improving, take time to rejoice in your successes. Set aside time to enjoy each other. Allow yourselves opportunities to do things together the way friends do. Why not stop right now and, in some special way, express your friendship to your father? It might be a physical expression (a hug and a kiss, for instance), it might be verbal (telling him how you feel), or your feelings might be expressed some other way (a note or a hot fudge sundae).

What a fortunate daughter you are to have such a good relationship with your father!

12.

Final Years: Tarnished Brass or Polished Gold?

There is a time for everything,
and a season for every activity under heaven:
a time to be born and a time to die.
—Ecclesiastes 3:1–2

"I remember when I got the phone call. It made my stomach do a somersault," Susanna said. "My mother called to tell me my father had just been diagnosed as having liver cancer. To me, my father was dependability personified. He had always been there for me, and I assumed he would be there forever."

"The worst thing about realizing that Dad really is an old man," says Daryl, "is that it reflects on me. If he's that old, then I must be getting old too. It's scary to think about."

An old Jewish proverb says, "Every man knows he will die, but no one wants to believe it." Perhaps no daughter wants to believe it of her father either. But unless your father is unfortunate enough to die young, the time will come when he will grow old and die.

Even though you know perfectly well this is a fact of life, it's often a shock when your father's growing dependency first becomes evident. Over a period of years, or sometimes all at once, your active, self-reliant father becomes physically limited and dependent. Suddenly, after a stroke, he is paralyzed. All at once, after complaining for years about your mumbling, you realize he can't hear a thing without his hearing aid. One day you realize his characteristic suspicion of people has become an obsession with hiding his wallet under his mattress. Poor concentration, memory loss, having trouble making decisions, aches and pains, problems with driving, fewer social contacts—all can make even the most independent aging dad turn to his daughter for help and support.

Sometimes, to make matters worse, he also becomes short-tempered, demanding, manipulative, and withdrawn. Already difficult fathers become even more difficult as they become more dependent. You may discover that unrecognized conflicts and resentments that have been dormant for years will suddenly reemerge as your relationship with your aging father takes up more of your time and attention.

Most frustrating of all is when you see all those old patterns you thought you had under control beginning to return, this time more powerfully than ever. You will surely be frustrated to see your hard-won progress toward your new relationship going down the drain. But the fact is, that's often what happens with advancing age. New gains are forgotten and old patterns reemerge. Tendencies grow stronger and take over. If your father used to be stubborn, he may now be absolutely immovable. If he was always suspicious, he may now be paranoid.

You remember your dad's words to you: "Don't worry about me. I'll never be a burden to you. The last thing I'll ever do is go to my children for help." But now here he is doing exactly what he swore he would never do.

In a last desperate effort to be forgiven for past mistakes or to prove that they really are the "good kid" of the family, some daughters respond to these effects of aging by bending over backwards to cater to their fathers' demands. Others react by denying that there ever was anything negative between themselves and their fathers.

CAUGHT IN THE MIDDLE

To make matters worse, at the same time that many of us are struggling to adjust to our aging parents, we are also contending with our maturing children. We are caught in the middle between the aging older generation and the emerging younger generation. While we are trying to explain the difficulties of our dads to our kids, we are at the same time apologizing to our fathers for our children's music, clothes, and hairstyles. We understand both sides, because we have one foot in each world. Yet here we are, caught in the middle of the biggest generation gap imaginable, struggling with all we've got to build a bridge over it between our fathers and our children. Now and then we are successful.

You may feel you are caught in a hopeless trap. How can you give your father what he needs and still be responsible toward your own family, if you have one? And how can you find any time to go about living your own life? It's frustrating to feel you have to do it all yet know you can't.

On the face of it, being caught in the middle seems awfully depressing, even hopeless. But it need not be. We can accept the challenge and creatively search for ways to help both our fathers and ourselves grow together in a way neither could alone.

ACCEPT AND PREPARE

"Not my father," Carrie thought. *"He won't grow old. He'll never have to depend on me. That happens to other people's dads, but not to mine.* I never actually said it, of course, because it isn't rational. But that's the way I felt."

And now?

"Now when I look at him, I'm sad. He *does* need me. It happened suddenly when my mom died. I wasn't prepared for it." Carrie paused for a minute then added, "Dad was always the strong one, the one with all the answers. Now he needs *my* strength. He looks to *me* for answers. It just doesn't seem right, does it?"

No, it doesn't seem right. Yet it happens.

I saw this quotation in an advertisement for a local retirement hotel: "The independence that we enjoy is different than the independence our parents endure." What a statement! If we are to make our fathers' final years as golden as possible, we need to accept the inevitable and prepare for it.

It does no good to deny what is happening. When your father stumbles and falters, you can't just brush it off with, "He just needs new glasses." Or when he forgets to turn the stove off yet again, you can't ignore it and say, "Everyone makes mistakes."

To deny and make excuses is just a way of saying, "I don't want to think about it. Not yet." But denial doesn't change anything. What it may do is keep you from seeking out the help that is available to you.

Old age is "the season of losses." Besides losing his memory capacity and other physical abilities, your father also may be losing his talents, his independence, and even worse, his friends. The circle of people who are important to him—his friends, family members, his wife—grows smaller and smaller with each passing year.

Ladder of Emotion

It is a wise daughter who prepares herself by planning how she will relate to her aging father. Carol Flax and Earl Ubell have developed what they call the Ladder of Emotion. The ladder is made up of eight rungs that represent eight levels of emotion you can expect to experience with your father. Knowing what to expect will help you decide the best way to relate to him, especially as he becomes more dependent and demanding. Consider the progression on the Ladder of Emotion:

1. I will listen to you.
2. I am interested in what you have to say.
3. I like you and am interested in what you have to say.
4. I like you and I want to help you.
5. I care for you and am interested in what you have to say.
6. I care for you and I want to help you.
7. I love you and am interested in what you have to say.
8. I love you and I want to help you.[1]

Do you see how this progress can relate to the way you listen to your father? Rungs 1–4 deal mainly with listening to facts. Rungs 5–8 show a deeper concern and a personal involvement.

Some fathers are unfortunately pretty hard to like. If yours is obstinate, unreasonable, angry, and hard to deal with, try to relate to him on your foundation of basic love, not on the way you feel right now.

Facing the Ultimate Loss

With each loss, with each illness, with each realization that yet another faculty is impaired will come another reason for your father to contemplate his own mortality. Many of us would be surprised to know that our elderly dads tend to accept the certainty of death more willingly than we do. When an aged parent wants to share his feelings about his death, his child often will respond with, "Don't even talk about that! You have lots of years left."

One eighty-six-year-old man said of his daughter, "I can't talk to her about death. She doesn't want the subject brought up. But I want to talk about it with her. I want to tell her what to do when I'm gone. She seems to think if we ignore it, I'll live forever. But I know I won't. I've lost too many friends. I know more about death than she does."

Not being able to talk to you about his concerns, fears,

and desires for what will be done after his death just increases your father's sense of isolation and loneliness. His concerns may seem needlessly negative or even scary to you. But that's not how he sees it.

Whether you are trying to cover up your own fears or protect your father, your unwillingness to talk about death often turns out to be a barrier to the love and communication you both need now more desperately than ever. In most cases, parents learn to avoid bringing up the painful subject of death. Many respond by retreating into isolation. What happens is that children of the dying parent are left without ever having had the chance to express their love.

Discussing death with your father can be an uncomfortable burden or it can be a special opportunity for intimacy. It is up to you to set the tone.

Where Will Your Father Spend the Last Part of His Life?

The time may come when you will decide your father can no longer live alone. Your first impulse may be to insist, "Come on, Dad, live with us!"

Don't move too quickly. While your intentions may be right on target, your decision might not be in your father's best interests—or in the best interest of your family. Maybe it won't even be in your best interest.

Before you act, step back and look at the situation from your dad's point of view. Ask yourself:

Does my father want to live with my family? He has a right to be involved in the decision.

Will he feel isolated in my home, without his own friends, church, organizations, or familiar surroundings? His adjustment will be all the more difficult if he feels isolated or lonely.

Is my home large enough to give him the privacy he needs? Will he be able to have a room of his own where he can have his belongings around him?

Now take a look from your family's point of view:

Will they be able to adjust to my father's presence? A three-generation household is a big undertaking for everyone.

Will my dad be able to manage by himself in my house? Before you answer this, consider your job or other commitments that take you away from home.

Is my husband as willing as I am to have my father move in? If not, the arrangement probably won't work.

Consider the move from your point of view:

How is my relationship with my father right now? Is it solid or is it tenuous? Is it well established or is it just beginning to emerge?

What is my motive for taking my dad in? If it is guilt, you will soon resent him for intruding into your home and your life.

As you consider such a move, encourage each member of your family to share his or her feelings about it. If everyone expresses honest emotions, your chances of working out the best arrangement for your father is much better. Of course, include your dad in the discussion. Be frank about what you might expect of him, both socially and in terms of responsibility and family chores. Also discuss the financial arrangements. When will your father be included in your activities? Will he feel hurt if you go out without him? Explain your needs to him and listen as he expresses his needs to you. Now is the time to understand each other thoroughly and completely.

If you are leaning toward having your father move in, it

might be a good idea to arrange for a trial period. If he is able, ask him to share in the household responsibilities—washing dishes or fixing things around the house. Allowing him to help may encourage him to feel like a needed family member instead of like a boarder. But remember, your dad is neither your servant nor your baby-sitter. Encourage him to invite his own friends to your home and to participate in his own outside activities. You will both be better off leading your own lives.

Don't be surprised if problems arise. Your dad may not be used to picking up his clothes or folding the newspaper back up when he finishes reading it. He may leave the bathroom faucet dripping or the cereal boxes open. He may criticize your kids. Or he may always have a better way of doing anything you happen to be doing. Ask yourself: Can I live with this on a long-term basis? Can everyone in the family adjust to this?

Allow yourself plenty of time to decide whether or not the move will work. Be sure everyone in the family understands what the issues are and has a chance to participate in the discussion.

Be open to everyone's perspective. "It wasn't working," Daryl said of the time her father first moved in with her family. "Dad was obsessed with helping. He followed me shopping and advised me on every purchase. He was with me in the kitchen every night, wanting to stir or taste or add more pepper. I know he just wanted to help, but he was driving me crazy.

"It was my five-year-old daughter Katie who finally came up with a solution. She said, 'Why can't Grandpa and me have some nights to cook?' So now, twice a week, Dad and Katie plan the meal together. They do the shopping, the cooking, and the cleaning up. Dad loves it, Katie loves it, and I love getting the nights off kitchen duty."

Sometimes, however, the arrangement just doesn't work out. "Dad tried and I tried," says Jeanette. "He was so determined not to be a burden. And he really was a good influence on my son during an especially difficult year of high school. Dad tried to help out in the kitchen, and he kept his room neat and clean. Even so, I was constantly asking my husband, 'When is he going to move out?' We both felt awkward with Dad there, and Dad seemed stiff and uncomfortable. We never planned it this way. It was as if our lives had been put on hold while we waited for Dad to make up his mind whether or not he was going to stay."

What Are Your Options?

What if it just doesn't work for your father to live with you? What then? Does he have to go into a nursing home?

Maybe. But before making such a decision, examine the entire situation. Is your father mentally alert? Can he care for his own needs—dressing, shopping, cooking? Does he need continual medical care? You may be able to find community resources that will allow him to keep living in his own home.

Check the alternatives: apartments adapted for the needs of the elderly, retirement hotels, public housing for senior citizens. Many offer such services as meals, resident or visiting medical personnel, recreation, and cultural programs suitable for the elderly. It may be that your dad will be able to live with a degree of self-sufficiency, yet be under the watchful eye of people who care about him.

Sometimes, however, a nursing home is the right answer. It may seem to be a frightening option, so exercise judgment and avoid making a decision you may later regret. If you have brothers and sisters, discuss the possibilities with them. If you act alone, you may be accused of doing the wrong things or of having selfish motives. It may also be that your siblings will think of good alternatives that never occurred to you.

Be sure that in all your planning and talking and weighing of options, you don't forget your dad. His participation is essential. Talk *with* him, not *at* him. Try asking his opinions rather than telling him what you have already decided. Choose a time when your father and everyone else is rested and in a good mood. Speak in gentle, calm tones rather than in a demanding or argumentative voice. Be willing to explain again and again without growing impatient.

It's important that your father understand the possible changes in his life. He may be cooperative and agreeable, or he may be angry and accusative. Whichever, be ready to sympathize with his reactions. This might be an excellent time to remind him of your love and respect for him. Assure him that you have no intention of abandoning him. You might say, "We don't have to make this decision right now" or "Whatever we decide, you will be part of the decision."

Such a time of change also will be a time of major stress for your father. Don't ignore this. On the other hand, don't underestimate your dad's ability to make a good adjustment. In fact, in his new environment he may actually be happier and more comfortable than he has been in years.

Listen to Him

If your dad feels that the whole world is against him, it's important for him to know that you, at least, are firmly on his side. You can go a long way toward demonstrating this by listening to what he has to say. He needs someone to talk to; let him know he can safely share his thoughts, feelings, and opinions with you. Don't interrupt him when he talks. If he rambles, listen to his rambling. If he says the same thing again and again, listen to it again and again. One word of caution, however: Letting your father talk doesn't mean *making* him talk, especially about things that are painful or embarrassing to him.

Be careful not to gloss over your father's complaints and worries with cheerful clichés and patronizing reassurances. If he says, "I don't feel well," don't say, "I just hope I'm as healthy as you when I'm your age." If he says, "I'm lonesome," don't respond with, "Get out and meet people. You have to be a friend to have a friend." If he hurts, he hurts. If he's lonely, he's lonely.

It's also important to complement your listening with sharing of your own. Open up your world to your father. Talk to him about your personal life, about things that are important to you. Ask his advice and let him know you value his ideas. He just might be able to help you with some of your own problems. It would be wonderful if, even for only a short time, he could feel like a parent again, to have something to offer someone he loves.

Acknowledge Him

Do you ever find yourself making decisions for your father? When the waitress asks him how he wants his eggs, do you say, "Scrambled"? At the doctor's office, do you answer when he is asked how he is feeling? Treating your father as if he's helpless can be devastating to him. It can destroy his assurance and whatever regard he has for himself.

When he is stubborn and impossible to reason with, ask yourself what you will gain by insisting or arguing. If he says, "I want a cheese sandwich," despite your insistence that he never liked cheese, what will it hurt to make him a cheese sandwich? Sometimes it's better to submit to him and avoid conflict. Your father may not be able to help what he's doing. He may not be capable of reason regardless of your insistence that he be reasonable. When you get angry and shout at him, you are the one who has lost control. Neither of you is a winner. As gently and lovingly as you can, try to decide what you can and can't reasonably expect of each other.

A sense of humor can be a lifesaver. Laughing—at yourself or the situation, not at your father—will relieve the tension and encourage your dad to laugh too. He may even be able to smile at himself.

And do remember the power of praise. When your dad is feeling low, your respect and admiration can lift him up. Your words and attitude can let him know he is still valued.

It may be that you and your dad haven't done much touching since you were very young. Yet touching is probably the most comforting way there is to communicate with another human being. Physical contact is witness to the quality of your feelings for your father. When there is nothing left to say, try holding his hands or giving him a hug.

Wherever your dad ends up living, whether with you or with another family member, whether in his own home or in a group facility, determine that you will provide him with the very best kind of love and care you can. If he is not living with you, give him as much attention as if he were. Better yet, give him more.

ACCENTUATE THE POSITIVE

It's not always easy to let those you love experience pain, frustration, or anger. You long to relieve your father's problems, even though you know it's necessary to let him find his own solutions. With time running out, it's important to savor your opportunities and to accentuate the positive.

Every human being in the world cries out, "I'm important! I'm special and unique! Watch me!" All of us want to be appreciated for who we are with our own needs and talents, our own strengths and weaknesses, our own possibilities. When those we love and trust help us to see ourselves as valuable, we bloom and prosper. We move forward, begin to set goals for ourselves, and hope bigger hopes than we ever dared before.

Your father's aging does not necessarily have to remove him from life. He can still live with purpose and meaning. By assisting him in changing the supports in his environment, you can help him maintain as much independence as possible. Those who make the best adjustment to old age are those who have outside interests, good social relationships with their families and relatives, a role in society, dignity, and some degree of independence.

Volunteering is a wonderful opportunity for your father to put his skills to use or even to learn different ones. It will allow him to come into contact with new people, new ideas, and new challenges. Many agencies incorporate positions for older volunteers. Volunteers are needed in schools, hospitals, day-care centers, churches, and clubs.

Another good outlet for your father is an adult-education program. Often these programs do more than just teach. They offer intellectual involvement, cultural stimulation, access to new friends, and a doorway to life beyond home.

What at first seems an end for your father—no more job, no more schedule to keep—can also be looked at as a beginning. Here is your father's chance to do all those things he never had time for before. And what about the things you and he always wanted to do together but never got around to trying? You can encourage your father by helping him take inventory. Together you can work at pinpointing his present needs and mapping out his future goals. Then you can encourage him to explore those activities that bring him the most enjoyment and satisfaction.

Speaking of encouragement, don't neglect the power in celebration. Praise your dad for his courage and his successes—even the little ones. When he wins at checkers, break out the rocky road ice cream. When he recovers from his bad cold, throw a little party. Celebrations let others know your father is around and that he deserves some notice. And it lets him know you're glad he's here.

Listening, sharing, touching, laughing, celebrating—these are exciting ways to create a loving atmosphere for your dad and yourself. And there's a side bonus to this plan: When you meet your father's needs, you just may end up meeting some of your own needs as well. When you reach out your hands to him, he just might reach back to you with his heart. As you help him end his days in love and respect, you just may find a new beginning within yourself.

An End

"I was twenty-six when my father died," LeeAnn says. "It was the sixteenth of August, the hottest day I ever remember. I got the news that night at my apartment in Los Angeles. It was so strange. All that day I had gone about my business, sitting in my air-conditioned office, eating lunch with my friend Renee at a salad bar, talking about office gossip, while my father was gasping his last breath in a little house in Wisconsin. It doesn't seem right. It happened too soon. How I wish I had had some warning. How I wish I had spent the time with him I always promised I would."

The wisdom of hindsight is painful because it is so filled with regrets. "At thirty-six, I cry for my father and myself as I couldn't when I was six or sixteen," LeeAnn continues. "But my feelings are so confused. Sometimes I'm so angry with him for dying that I bang my fists into my pillow. But then I remember the good times between us and I can do nothing but cry."

We daughters are never done with our fathers, even when they are no longer here. If your dad dies unexpectedly, you will be glad that you worked on your relationship with him. If he lives a long life, you still win, for you will have that many more years of friendship.

13.
Bylaws for Daughters

Friendship with your father—what an exciting goal! To be able to bridge the gap between yourself and your dad. To see that man who was once the most significant man in your life once again move into a position of being dear and important to you.

As you reach out to your father, you probably will find him ready and willing to reach back to you. Even if he doesn't reach back—if he isn't capable of doing so—your reach alone will bring the two of you closer together. In reaching out to him, you can't lose.

In this book you have read many suggestions drawn from various sources. I have shared ideas from a number of women of different ages and varied circumstances. I have also shared some guidelines for action. These suggestions, ideas, and guidelines can be summed up in a list of bylaws for daughters.

If you are committed to forming a lifetime friendship with your father, you might want to go over these ideas once again and put them to work for you.

Understand Your Relationship

Where are you and your father now? Unless you know where you are starting from, how can you know where you are going? And unless you know where you are going, how will you know when you get there? Any trip is easier if you have a map to follow. Examine the relationship that exists between you and your dad right now and decide the specific ways in which you would like to see it change.

Share Perspectives

When your father does or says something that bothers you a little, overlook it. If he does or says something that bothers you a lot, talk to him about it. Give him a chance to see the matter from your point of view. Then give him the opportunity to help you see it from his. It just may be that your dad will switch over to your side. If so, the problem is solved. Or you may see that his side isn't so bad after all, that it's a position with which you can live. If your father refuses to change and if he still drives you crazy, at least you will both know for sure where the other stands.

Share Expectations

Work toward the goal of understanding your father's expectations of you. Understand your expectations of him. Now decide, which of these are realistic? Which are not? Which are worth working on with your dad? First examine your expectations, then do some adjusting.

Get to Know Your Father

I know, I know. You think you have known him your entire life. But I mean, really get to *know* him. What were his parents like? What were their expectations of him? How was his background different from yours? What causes him to say the things he says, to do the things he does, to hold the opinions he holds, to cling to his causes? Do you see traits of him in yourself? Do you see areas in which you are different? Get to *know* him.

Find Out What's Important to Him

Take the trouble to find out what is important to him. If you don't know this, how can you really talk to him on his level? How can you ever hope to see things from his perspective? You can't expect him to be interested in your life and your interests when you care little about his.

Admit Your Dad Isn't Perfect

For some daughters, this is a hard step. A daughter who is used to seeing her father as the perfect man will have trouble seeing beyond him. On the other hand, a daughter who has for years dwelt on her father's weaknesses and failures may have a hard time looking at him without criticizing. Learn to accept your father's faults while maximizing his strengths.

Accept Your Differences

You and your dad are different. That's as it should be. Your father is entitled to his own opinions, and he doesn't owe you an apology for them. Accept the fact that you don't have to agree on everything in order to be friends. As with any other friend, be willing to overlook and accept and adapt.

Give Him the Benefit of the Doubt

Your dad may be the type who has an opinion about everything. You may be tired of hearing the same old things again and again and again. Though you certainly don't want him to remind you of it one more time, he *is* older than you are. He *has* lived longer. He probably *does* have insights beyond yours. He really may have something to teach you. Assume that listening to him is worth your while. Try to hear beyond the "way he always says it" to what he is saying.

Learn to Communicate

Don't talk *at* your father. Don't even talk *to* him. Talk *with* him. There's a huge difference between the three, you know. No matter how unreasonable your dad is, no matter how stubborn and inflexible, no matter how determined he is that he is right, keep your conversations two-sided. When you share, do it thoughtfully. When you listen, listen beneficially. When your father talks to you, try to hear what is behind his words. Listen for his feelings. Listen to *him*. That is, after all, what communication is all about.

Share Your Attention with Your Father

Make the effort to be with your dad, to include him in family activities, to help him to feel truly useful. My father is never happier than when I have put aside a collection of things he can fix for me. He loves to use his hands. He's good at it, and he wants to be helpful. What can you depend on your father to do for you?

If you have children, they can learn a lot by getting to know their grandfather. When they are little, they will enjoy his stories and his attention. As they grow older, you may find that it's actually easier for them to relate to Grandpa than to you. Whatever their age, they have the opportunity to learn lessons of love, patience, and compassion from being with him.

Allow Your Father Time Alone

Encourage your father to be with his own friends, to pursue his own interests, or to just be alone. Both of you need time apart from each other. If he tends to follow you around and cling to you, tell him kindly but firmly that it is important for you and for him to go your separate ways at times. You may be surprised to find that this is actually a relief to him!

Learn to Handle Conflict, Anger, and Criticism

No matter how close you and your father are, conflict will sometimes occur. For most of us, conflict will happen more often than we care to admit. At times you are sure to get angry at him. Your dad may have habits and behavior patterns that drive you to the end of your rope. But knowing that conflicts, anger, and criticisms are bound to occur enables you to think ahead about how you will respond when they come. If certain situations are a frequent problem between you and your father, you might want to plan out specific comments and examples to use when they arise.

Give Your Relationship a High Priority

Let your dad know your relationship really is important to you. Tell him you are determined to stick with your resolve to strengthen and rebuild it. If the going gets rough, refuse to give up. Keep working, keep praying, and keep expecting positive results.

Be Willing to Take the Initiative

Most daughters want to be friends with their fathers. Some choose to wait for their relationship to improve spontaneously. Others are determined to hold back until their fathers make the first move. It's unlikely that either will happen. If you truly want a new, improved, healthy relationship with your dad, you will have to take the initiative. You will have to make it happen.

Let Your Father Live His Own Life

Many daughters find it much easier to insist on their own privacy than to allow the same consideration to their fathers. Your dad doesn't owe you an explanation for everything he does. He also is an adult, and he has been one considerably longer than you have. Respect his privacy and his right to a life of his own. Encourage him to develop his own hobbies and friendships. Unless his condition requires it, don't continually call to check up on him. Don't expect him to keep you informed about what he does, when he does it, and with whom. If you try to control your father's life, he is sure to resent it—and you too.

Help Your Father Stay Independent

Whenever possible, let your dad lead his life without too much interference from you. He will be much happier to have you around if it is on his terms. Making your father dependent on you before it's absolutely necessary will be doing yourself—and him—no favor. Even though it may take time and patience on your part, give your dad the dignity of doing things for himself just as long as he can.

Be Patient with Him

Don't expect your father to change overnight. His patterns of behavior are deeply ingrained. If you start out expecting the process of change to take time, you won't be so easily discouraged when it doesn't happen all at once.

Be Slow to Correct

It's so easy to get into the habit of constantly jumping in to correct your father. But would it really be so terrible to let some of his mistakes go unnoticed? Most of the time it doesn't really matter that much anyway. Don't expect perfection from him and maybe he will be gracious enough to allow you the same leeway. Remember, your father is not a child to be corrected and trained. He's a full-grown adult, the one who raised you. Be content just to love him and to enjoy having him around.

Watch, too, that you don't criticize him in front of his friends. To do so will be humiliating to him. Whenever possible, hold your advice until your father asks for it.

Build Up Your Dad

Affirming your father's cooperation whenever possible will deepen your friendship with him. Most likely, building a better relationship was your idea. He may have thought things were just fine the way they were. When you recognize gestures that indicate he appreciates what is going on between you, tell him how much you appreciate him. You might even punctuate it by giving him a hug and a kiss.

Compliment Him

Compliment your dad often. Be quick to say "thank you." It's so easy to assume that a kind gesture or a thoughtful word requires so little time or effort that it really isn't worth much. You may be right or you may be wrong. Either way, your father will appreciate having you express your gratitude. "I love you" and "You mean so much to me" and "I appreciate the way you listen to me even when you don't agree" and "It's so nice to have you around" are powerfully effective words. Pepper your conversation with these kinds of statements and you are sure to be surprised at the response you will get.

Enjoy Your Friendship

Fathers and daughters were meant to be friends. Unfortunately, it doesn't happen automatically. It takes time, patience, effort, and determination. It takes faith, trust, hope, and love.

Is it easy to make friends with your father? For a few daughters, yes. But not for most of us.

"The principle of friendship is a good one," Jeanette says. "I've always thought so. Making it happen, though, was hard. But I stuck with it."

And now?

"Now we are friends, my dad and me," she says with a smile. "And my father was worth every bit of the time and trouble. He says the same about me."

That's how it is between fathers and daughters who care.

Notes

CHAPTER 4—PROBLEM FATHERS
[1]H. Norman Wright, *Always Daddy's Girl* (Ventura, Calif.: Regal, 1989), 146–47.

CHAPTER 5—DADS WHO WEREN'T THERE
[1]H. Norman Wright, *Always Daddy's Girl* (Ventura, Calif.: Regal, 1989), 89.

CHAPTER 6—GOD, THE FATHER
[1]William and Kristi Gaultiere, *Mistaken Identity* (Old Tappan, N.J.: Revell, 1989), 56.

CHAPTER 7—CHANGING YOUR FATHER'S EFFECT ON YOU
[1]William and Kristi Gaultiere, *Mistaken Identity* (Old Tappan, N.J.: Revell, 1989), 95.

CHAPTER 11—YOUR FATHER, YOUR FRIEND
[1]Carol Flax and Earl Ubell, *Mother, Father, You* (Ridgefield, Conn.: Wyden Books, 1989), 192–201.

CHAPTER 12—FINAL YEARS: TARNISHED BRASS OR POLISHED GOLD?
[1]Carol Flax and Earl Ubell, *Mother, Father, You* (Ridgefield, Conn.: Wyden Books, 1989), 184.

Bibliography

Bloomfield, Harold H., M.D., and Felder, Leonard. *Making Peace with Your Parents*. Bloomfield Productions, 1983.

Flax, Carol, and Ubell, Earl. *Mother, Father, You*. Ridgefield, Conn.: Wyden Books, 1989.

Gaultiere, William and Kristi. *Mistaken Identity*. Old Tappan, N.J.: Revell, 1989.

Halpern, Howard. *Cutting Loose*. New York: Bantam, 1977.

Strom, Kay Marshall. *Making Friends with Your Mother*. Grand Rapids: Zondervan, 1991.

_____. *Perfect in His Eyes*. Grand Rapids: Zondervan, 1988.

Woolfolk, William, and Cross, Donna. *Daddy's Little Girl*. Englewood Cliffs, N.J.: Prentice-Hall, 1982.

Wright, H. Norman. *Always Daddy's Girl*. Ventura, Calif.: Regal, 1989.